Traditional English Food

A TASTE
OF ENGLAND

Theodora FitzGibbon

Period photographs specially prepared by

George Morrison

Pan Books London and Sydney

for our good friends Rosemary and Mark Booth
and Maureen and Will Hoyle, with many thanks
for all the help they gave us.

Also in this series by Theodora FitzGibbon in Pan Books

A Taste of Ireland
A Taste of Scotland
A Taste of Wales
A Taste of the West Country
A Taste of London
A Taste of Yorkshire
A Taste of the Lake District

First published 1986 by Pan Books Ltd,
Cavaye Place, London SW10 9PG
9 8 7 6 5 4 3 2 1
© Theodora FitzGibbon 1986
ISBN 0 330 29169 6
Photoset by Parker Typesetting Service, Leicester
Printed and bound in Great Britain by
Richard Clay (The Chaucer Press) Ltd, Bungay, Suffolk

ACKNOWLEDGEMENTS

On this memorable journey of over three thousand miles we met many old friends and made many new ones, to all of whom we express our deepest thanks: particularly to Nancy, Lady Bagot for her photographs, Mr Niall MacSwiggan, Mrs Artingstall in Lymm, and my old friend Moira Lyle for endless hospitality and books. To the friends to whom we have dedicated this book it is impossible to say how much we owe to them in finding photographs and old books.

Our thanks are also due to the staff of the many museums, libraries and record offices we visited who were helpful during our researches. Photographs on pages 6, 73, 98 are reproduced by kind permission of Mr Robin Gard, of the Northumberland Record Office; on page 8 is from the Warrington Museum and Art Gallery; to the Cambridge Central Library we are grateful for photographs on pages 22, 50, 153; on pages 14, 26, 62, with kind permission of Mr David Wall, Chelmsford Public Library; on pages 29, 37, 54, 61, 74, 93, 106, 113, 114, 129, 137, we thank very much Richard Chamberlaine Brothers and Mark Booth, also Mrs Rosemary Booth for her contribution on pages 34, 105, 121; many thanks to Dr William Allan of Warwickshire County Museum for the photograph on page 41; we thank the Suffolk Record Office for photographs on pages 30, 57, 134; thanks are due to Mr Stephen Best and his staff at Nottingham Library for photographs on pages 42, 117, 146; and to Mr Halfpenny at Wedgwood Works, Etruria for the photograph on page 45; to Beamish Hall Museum on page 46; thanks to Mr Paul Ellis and Miss Margaret Sanders of Worcester City Library for photographs on pages 49, 149; and particularly to

Mr Douglas Tideswell of Northwich for his family's photograph of the Northwick salt mines; Mary Burkett OBE of Abbot Hall Museum, Kendal for the photograph on page 66; Colman's Mustard of Norwich were most helpful with photographs for which we thank them; thanks to the Carnegie Central Library, Harrogate for the photograph on page 77; to the Newarke Houses Museum, Leicester for the photograph on page 78; grateful thanks to the Dean and Chapter, Durham Cathedral for the photographs on pages 21, 89; to Lea & Perrins, Worcester for their photograph and books on page 90; to Miss Hebden, Hereford and Worcester County Library, Malvern for the photograph on page 133; and Miss Bowen of Derby Local Studies Library for the photographs on pages 94, 102, 126; finally Aberdeen Central Library for photographs on pages 70, 81, 130, 153.

INTRODUCTION

To travel through the whole of England is to realize what a rich and varied country it is. There is so much beauty, both grand and awe-inspiring as well as small hidden corners, often overlooked in travel books, which have a charm not easily forgotten. In space it is small compared to many other countries, yet you are left with the impression of a vast canvas upon which many deft hands have painted. From one county to the next you could be on a different island, this being particularly true of the east and west coasts, the north of England and the south. Although parts are very industrialized, within the space of a few miles you are in the depths of the country again. Some counties, like the Lake District of Cumbria, seem almost untouched for the last fifty years. The glorious lakes, the imposing mountains and their protected valleys, must surely look very much as they did when Wordsworth and the Lake poets lived there.

The people, too, change from county to county and one realizes the truth in Daniel Defoe's poem, *The True-born Englishman*, which ends with these telling lines:

'By which, with easy search you may distinguish
Your Roman-Saxon-Danish-Norman English.
Fate jumbled them together – God knows how!
Whate'er they were – they're true-born English now.'

With such a history, as you can imagine, the food from place to place varies too. The thick clotted cream of Cornwall and Devonshire does not travel far from where it is made, any more than the succulent Cumberland sausage leaves Cumbria. The wildfowl of the fens do not mingle with the fat Aylesbury ducklings and Lincolnshire stuffed chine also stays at home. The English are rightly proud of their heritage and today, amongst the welter of take-aways and fast food places, they are even more determined to keep it alive. Traditions sometimes connected with food are not lost either.

It is impossible to write about all the great men and women that England has produced, in a book of this length, but in every county can be found some outstanding figure who has contributed to knowledge and beauty, known all over the world. As the title implies, this is only a taste of England, but other books in this series look at some regions in detail.

It is not a country to hurry through, but to savour, take slowly and remember. The Reverend Sydney Smith (1771–1845), the witty, food-loving canon of St Paul's wrote:

'I am convinced that character, talents, virtues and qualities are powerfully affected by beef, mutton, pie crust and rich soups.'

Theodora FitzGibbon,
Atlanta,
Dalkey, Co. Dublin,
Ireland,
1985.

TWEED KETTLE

This border town has changed hands thirteen times in 300 years, but is now English. It has three handsome bridges, the Royal Border being built in 1850 by Robert Stephenson, George Stephenson's son. There are extensive Elizabethan town walls which were a model for others of their day. It is now a resort with all amenities and good fishing.

TWEED KETTLE

Salmon from the Tweed river is well known for its flavour and the traditional methods of cooking preserve that delicacy. The pan in which the salmon is cooked is always called a fish kettle.

900 g (2 lb) fresh salmon, middle cut or tail end	1 shallot or small onion, chopped
salt and pepper	3 tablespoons white wine vinegar
pinch of nutmeg	
water	2 tablespoons parsley, chopped

Serves about 6

See that the fish is cleaned, retaining any liver or roe which should be cooked separately and used as garnish. Put into a fish kettle or large saucepan and cover with cold water, salt and pepper. Bring slowly to the boil and cook gently for about 10 minutes. Leave in the liquid until cool, but reserve 300 ml (½ pint) of fish stock when you are draining it. Lift out gently, skin and bone thoroughly.

Cut into 2.5 cm (1 in) strips and put back in pan in the shape of the fish. Add the reserved liquid, nutmeg, shallot, wine vinegar, salt and pepper. Bring gently to the boil and simmer for about 20 minutes. Serve with some of the liquid and the parsley, either hot or cold.

RAILWAY PUDDING

A 19th-century pudding served with lemon sauce.

100 g (4 oz) butter	225 g (8 oz) self-raising flour
100 g (4 oz) castor sugar	50 g (2 oz) currants
2 eggs	a little butter

Serves about 4

Cream butter and sugar until light. Beat in eggs and add flour and currants. Well grease an ovenproof dish and preheat oven to 190°C, 375°F, Gas Mark 5. Bake for 20–25 minutes.

TO MAKE THE LEMON SAUCE: mix 12 g (½ oz) cornflour with a little water. Boil rest of 300 ml (½ pint) water and 100 g (4 oz) sugar for 3 minutes. Stir in cornflour with grated rind of 1 lemon and the strained juice. Simmer for 2 minutes stirring all the time. Orange sauce can be made by substituting orange for lemon.

Train coming into Berwick-upon-Tweed Station, Northumberland, with tea-trolley waiting, c. 1901.

BATCHELOR'S BUTTONS

Cheltenham was just a Cotswold village until 1715. Then a mineral spring was discovered, when some very healthy pigeons were seen to be drinking from it. True or not, Cheltenham does include a pigeon on its crest! In 1783 a Captain Henry Skillicorne set up a pump room there and it became established as a fashionable spa, popularized by George III who was a frequent visitor. These waters can be drunk today at the Town Hall as well as the Pump Room.

Many literary figures have stayed there, including Fanny Burney, who wrote about it in her diary, Tennyson and James Elroy Flecker.

BATCHELOR'S BUTTONS

A little biscuity-cake hardly ever seen today but which was a favourite for tea in the last century and in the early years of this one.

100 g (4 oz) butter	2 teaspoons bicarbonate soda
225 g (8 oz) flour	2 small eggs
1 teaspoon cream of tartar	approx. 2 tablespoons demerara
75 g (3 oz) sugar	sugar

Makes about 30 small cakes

Mix together all dry ingredients, except demerara sugar then work in the butter until it is like fine breadcrumbs. Add the beaten eggs and mix to a smooth paste. Preheat oven to 180°C, 350°F, Gas Mark 4 and lightly grease a baking sheet.

Roll the mixture into small balls about the size of a large walnut, then roll each ball in the demerara sugar. Put them on the baking sheet a little apart and bake for about 10–15 minutes.

RAISIN TEA LOAF

100 g (4 oz) wheatmeal flour	1 egg, large
100 g (4 oz) self-raising flour	approx. 150 ml ($\frac{1}{4}$ pint) mixed
225 g (8 oz) raisins	milk and water
2 tablespoons melted butter	
2 tablespoons golden syrup, melted	

Lightly grease a 450 g (1 lb) loaf tin and preheat oven to 180°C, 350°F, Gas Mark 4.

Mix all dry ingredients and fruit. Warm syrup and add, then melted butter and beaten egg. Add the milk and water gradually until it is a firm dough. Put into the prepared tin and bake for 45–60 minutes.

Carriage in front of Queen's Hotel, Cheltenham, Gloucestershire, c. 1910.

SOUTHPORT PUDDING

Southport is an elegant northern resort with a covered colonnade of excellent shops in Lord Street, a fine pier, and six miles of sandy beach once used for motor racing. At the end of the 18th century Southport was just a collection of fishermen's huts until in 1835 the building of Lord Street was undertaken.

Eccles cakes would certainly have been on sale in the amusement park at this time (see page 155) as well as 'Barms' which are baps usually filled with sliced beef, i.e. Beef Barms, and a sandwich loaf is known as 'Rasps'.

garine, then add all the dry ingredients and peel. Add the lemon rind and juice mixing well. Beat the egg with the milk and stir in, folding it in very thoroughly. Press down into the greased basin, cover with buttered greaseproof paper or foil and tie down. Steam over boiling water for 2 hours.

Hold a warmed serving plate over the top when the papers have been removed and invert quickly. Serve with the lemon sauce.

SOUTHPORT PUDDING

2 cooking apples, about 100 g (4 oz), chopped
75 g (3 oz) shredded suet or margarine
50 g (2 oz) self-raising flour
50 g (2 oz) sugar
½ teaspoon nutmeg
100 g (4 oz) fresh white breadcrumbs
grated rind of ½ lemon and the juice
25 g (1 oz) candied peel, chopped
1 egg, large
approx. 4 tablespoons milk
a little butter for greasing
lemon sauce (see page 7)

Serves 4–6

Butter a 900 ml (1½ pint) pudding basin. Core the apples and chop them without peeling, very finely. Add the suet or melted mar-

RICE CAKES

100 g (4 oz) butter
100 g (4 oz) sugar
2 eggs, beaten
75 g (3 oz) self-raising flour
40 g (1½ oz) ground rice or rice flour
good squeeze of lemon

Makes 18 cakes

Grease 18 patty pans. Cream the butter and sugar until light, add the well-beaten eggs, then sift the two flours and stir in lightly. Add the lemon juice and mix well. Put into prepared tins and bake in a preheated oven at 200°C, 400°F, Gas Mark 6 for 10 minutes, then reduce heat to 190°C, 375°F, Gas Mark 5 and cook for a further 7–10 minutes. To test if they are done press the centre lightly, when ready it should spring back again easily.

The 'Flying Machine' at the Amusement Park, Southport, Lancashire (now Merseyside) 1909.

GOOSEBERRY FOOL

Morris Dancing in its present form dates back to the 15th century and is thought to be named after the Spanish morisca, meaning a Moorish dance. However, it probably goes back much further and may be a survival of a pre-Christian ceremony of sacrificial spring dances that took place throughout Europe. In many parts of England, the May Queen festival is also accompanied by Morris Dancers and traditional plays, as well as dancing round the maypole. Both celebrated the fertile transition into summer. May Day was superimposed on Beltane, which is when the Celts marked the beginning of summer with large bonfires in honour of the Sun-God. See also Whalton Baal Ceremony, page 46.

In Lymm, the ceremony with the May Queen takes place on the first Saturday in June. In the photograph, the man in the middle is the Fool (Ned Rowles) who led the group. They were also one of two groups in the Rushbearing ceremonies held on the first Monday after the second Sunday in August. (See also page 66.) The other group came from Thelwall which continued in being after the Lymm Dancers had disbanded. These ceremonies are still continued here. Eccles cakes (page 155) are eaten at this festival.

GOOSEBERRY FOOL

Excellent gooseberries are grown in Cheshire and also further north in England. There are many competitions for good gooseberries all over the county and the title of world champion gooseberry grower was awarded some years ago to a Cheshire man.

450 g (1 lb) gooseberries
100 g (4 oz) sugar
a few elderflower heads

300 ml ($\frac{1}{2}$ pint) double cream
1–2 egg whites, beaten stiffly

Serves 4–6

Top and tail the gooseberries and cook them in about 3–4 tablespoons of water with the sugar, until they are soft. At the last minute plunge in the elderflower heads tied together and leave for about 7–10 minutes, then lift them out. This gives the gooseberries a lovely scented flavour. Leave to cool and meanwhile whip the cream and the egg white(s) separately. Sieve or liquidize the gooseberries until they are a purée, taste for sugar, then stir in the cream and finally the egg white(s). Serve either in one large dish, or in individual glasses or dishes.

Morris Dancers at the Bazaar, corner of Henry Street, Lymm, Cheshire, c.1910 (photographer C. E. Ardern).

OYSTER SOUP

When the Roman emperor Claudius entered Colchester in AD 43 it had been an inhabited site for about 1,000 years. It was then called *Camulodunum* which was Shakespeare's *Cymbeline*. Colchester oysters were enjoyed very much by the Romans and it seems they took some back to Italy, for Colne river oyster shells have been found in ruins there. Pliny, the Roman historian is said to have maintained: 'the only good thing about England is its oysters'. Indeed Colchester oysters are still held in high esteem all over the world today. There is an oyster festival held there in October, at the Moot Hall.

'On this shore also are taken the best and nicest, though not the largest oysters in England: ... the chief other sort of fish which they carry from this part of the shore to London, are soles, which they take sometimes exceeding large.' (A Tour through the Whole Island of Great Britain, Daniel Defoe, 1724–6.)

OYSTER SOUP

It seems almost a shame to cook these delicious little morsels, but I remember with so much pleasure this creamy, delicious soup.

2 dozen fresh oysters (canned will do but are not so good for flavour)
50 g (2 oz) butter
2 level tablespoons flour
600 ml (1 pint) hot milk
parsley to garnish
$\frac{1}{2}$ teaspoon anchovy essence
a pinch each of nutmeg and cayenne
freshly ground white pepper
300 ml ($\frac{1}{2}$ pint) cream
lemon juice

Serves about 4–6

Get the oysters opened, reserving any juice. Melt the butter, stir in the flour and cook for 2 minutes. Gradually add the hot milk, stirring all the time until smooth and creamy. Then add the anchovy essence and the nutmeg and cayenne pepper. Add the cream and bring up to just simmering and keep it at that heat for about 25 minutes. Taste for seasonings.

Just before serving, add the oysters and their juice and *don't* overcook them or they will become rubbery. They should just start to curl. Add a good squeeze of lemon juice and serve straight away garnished with parsley. Do not keep it hot: if guests are late then add the oysters just before serving.

This soup can also be made with mussels, or a mixture of oysters and mussels and other shellfish.

Fish and poulterers shop on Shiregate Steps, Colchester, Essex, 1908.

LINCOLNSHIRE STUFFED CHINE

These cars were touring Britain with £5,000 of cinematographic equipment showing how the cars were made. Lincoln Cathedral, up high on a hill, was started by the Normans in 1072 when Bishop Remigius moved the seat of his diocese to Lincoln. The Norman work under the third bishop can still be seen on the west front. After a fire in 1141 it was finished in the mid-13th century, and the central tower in 1311. The Wren library was added in the 17th century and contains one of the four original copies of the Magna Carta.

LINCOLNSHIRE STUFFED CHINE

This is a particularly Lincolnshire dish made from a cut of bacon known in these parts. The chine is cut from between the shoulder blades across the backbone and can only be done with a joint from a butcher who does his own cutting. A. W. Curtis and Sons of Lincoln will supply these joints. When Verlaine, the French poet, spent a year as a schoolteacher at Boston, Lincolnshire, he was extremely fond of it, as was Tennyson, a native of Lincolnshire. It was served on Mothering Sunday and Trinity Sunday and for special occasions, like christenings.

1 chine bacon, soaked overnight   about 6 spring onions
2 cups of finely chopped parsley
½ cup chopped marjoram &
   thyme

Soak the meat overnight, drain and pat dry. Turn the fat side of the meat towards you and including a border of meat make deep slashes, about 5 or 6 in all, along the joint to half-way down, then turn round and do the same on the other side. Then chop or process the herbs, but do not pulverize them too much, they should be just moist. Add the finely chopped spring onions too, mixing well. Stuff these herbs into the slashes (you will see why you want them very fine), cramming in as much as you can, but even them off on both sides.

Tie the joint in a cloth tightly, put into a pan with cold water to cover and simmer for 3½–4 hours depending on the size. If water gets salty change it. Cool in the water for a few hours, then take out, and with the cloth still on, press under a weight overnight. Then unwrap and slice from the fat end parallel to the fat and reassemble for serving. It is eaten with vinegar and mustard. But in Clee on Trinity Sunday these pancakes are served with it.

CLEE SAUCER PANCAKES

450g (1 lb) rich shortcrust (page 76) is rolled and 8 buttered ovenproof saucers lined. Then 225g (8oz) curds are mixed well with 100g (4oz) sugar, salt, nutmeg, grated rind of ½ lemon and 6 egg yolks. This is spread over the pastry and sprinkled with chopped citron peel and baked at 190°C, 375°F, Gas Mark 5 for 30 minutes until golden. Serve hot.

South porch of Lincoln Cathedral with Flanders and E. M. F's cars touring Britain, c. 1910. (Photographer, H. Walker.)

WILD DUCK

Game is plentiful in this part of England, particularly pheasant, which is often on the menu at the excellent pub The Wig and Mitre, Lincoln, also wild duck.

The fenland of Lincolnshire extends for many miles to the Norfolk border. Much of it has been drained and now grows first class vegetables and flowers.

WILD DUCK

Wild duck should be hung for a week before cooking, unless cooked the same day they are shot. This recipe will also be good for widgeon or teal but as they are much smaller birds they will only need about half the cooking time. Contrary to what some people think, wild duck do not taste fishy, for their diet consists mostly of weeds and algae.

2 wild duck	salt and black pepper
4 rashers streaky bacon	1 tablespoon lemon juice
3–4 tablespoons oil or butter	cayenne pepper
8 tablespoons port wine (or red wine)	1 teaspoon mushroom ketchup
	2 tablespoons brandy, warmed

Serves about 4

Cover the breasts of the birds with the bacon, put into a roasting dish with the oil or butter and then cook in a preheated oven at 200°C, 400°F, Gas Mark 6 for about 30 minutes. Lower heat to 180°C, 350°F, Gas Mark 4 for about 15 minutes after basting.

Lift off the bacon and roll it up to be used as a garnish, take out the birds and put them on to a warmed dish. Score along the breastbone 2 or 3 times and sprinkle each score with a little cayenne, salt and pepper and lemon juice.

Pour off any fat from the dish and add the port and mushroom ketchup to the juices, mixing well. Taste for seasoning. Then put the birds back on top of the stove, baste with this gravy and reheat them. Put the brandy in a ladle and heat it up over a flame, then set fire to it and pour over the birds, flaming. Serve as soon as possible after this with some fresh watercress, game chips and the sauce, separately.

Other Lincolnshire recipes are on page 16.

Punt with gun for wild-fowling in the Lincolnshire fens, Cowbit (pronounced Cubbit), 1900. (Photographer, Canon Hubert Larker.)

ORANGE PUDDING

'Residence dinners at Durham Cathedral have been described or mentioned by several writers . . . Their origin is in the statutes issued to the Dean and Chapter by Queen Mary in 1555. These statutes are in most respects a very mild revision of the draft statutes issued by Henry VIII to most of the cathedrals of his new foundation, but the Durham statutes devote much more space to residence. At Durham the Dean, and every Canon who had £40 or more a year from a source outside the cathedral, was required to maintain a separate household, to keep residence and to provide hospitality. Residence in this context meant a period of twenty-one consecutive days each year. Many of the members of the chapter were not always pleased with the cost of this entertaining, but others seemed to enjoy it. In 1795 Canon Bouyer's plan for the table was: '. . . a salver in the centre and around it dishes holding soup, white collops, "regoltes", tongue, tartlets, blancmange, pasties, fillet of mutton, jelly, stewed beef, celery, "cold pot", asparagus, chickens, turkey, potted lobster, beetroot, ham, marinade of pork, orange jelly, pudding, lamb cutlets and fricasse – a total of twenty-eight dishes . . . The removes, or second courses, were fish, a chine of mutton, wild ducks, venison, a quarter of lamb and a pig. A side table carried a round of beef and vegetables and for dessert there were two rows of 11 unspecified dishes and one of nine.' All for twenty-four people! 'The residence dinners faded out in the second quarter of the 19th century, a period of revolutionary change when, as George Waddington, Dean of Durham from 1840, put it: "What with diner à la Russe, crinoline and pale sherry, England is fast going to the dogs."' (From: Hospitality Residence at Durham Cathedral, by Patrick Mussett, 1982.)

HOW TO MAKE AN ORANGE PUDDING

From Thacker's Art of Cookery 1758.

Take four Naples biscuits*, grate them fine; boil a pint of cream and a pint of milk together; put it to your biscuits, and sweeten to your taste; grate in the rind of a Seville orange and squeeze in the juice; colour it with a little saffron, tied up in a fine cloth, and soaked in 3 or 4 spoonfuls of Sack or orange-flower water, which put into your pudding, then slice in half a candied orange peel; and beat 8 eggs fine; strain them and grate in half a nutmeg; put in a little salt; mince the marrow-half of a marrow bone, or a quarter of a pound of melted butter, which put in, and mix all together, butter your dish; fill it and put a border of puff paste around.

*NAPLES BISCUITS

Take 4 eggs. Divide the whites from the yolks into separate bowls. Beat the yolks well and mix with these 100 g (4 oz) castor sugar, a pinch of salt, 2 or 3 drops of almond essence, 25 g (1 oz) flour and 37 g (1½ oz) cornflour. Mix to a smooth batter, then add whites whisked to a froth. Bake in a moderate oven in fingers, sprinkled with sugar, until pale.

The Deanery Kitchen, Durham Cathedral, Durham, c. 1900. (By kind permission of the Dean and Chapter.)

CAMBRIDGE CREAM

Trinity College Cambridge was founded in 1546 by King Henry VIII, and absorbed several earlier 14th-century institutions. It is entered from Trinity Street by the King's Gateway (1518–35) preserved from the King's Hall which was founded by Edward III in 1336 but subsequently altered.

Trinity College is responsible for some good recipes, notably a Cider Cup and a rich and delicious pudding.

CAMBRIDGE CREAM

Also called Burnt Cream and Crème Brulée. It has an amusing history in Cambridge related by the sister of a former Cambridge University librarian. Apparently, the recipe came from an Aberdeenshire country house (no doubt garnered from the admirable Mrs Cleland's *A New and Easy Method of Cookery* published in Scotland, 1759), was brought to the kitchens of Trinity College by an undergraduate, and rejected with contempt. In due time this undergraduate became a Fellow in 1879 and he presented it again when it was accepted as a matter of course! It rapidly became a favourite for May Week served with the strawberries Cambridgeshire is famous for.

Sweeping the snow from King's Gateway, Trinity College, Cambridge, 1891.

6 egg yolks
225 g (8 oz) castor sugar

600 ml (1 pint) double cream, or half-double and half-single cream

Serves 4–6

Beat the egg yolks with a tablespoon of sugar and pour the cream into a pan, bring to the boil and pour over the eggs in the bowl whisking all the time. It is easier to transfer to a double boiler or put a basin over hot, not boiling, water as the mixture must on no account boil. Heat the mixture gently until it thickens and coats the back of a wooden spoon.

Pour into a fairly shallow, heat-proof dish and leave to chill overnight. Two hours before it is needed, sprinkle the cream with an even layer of the sugar and pre-heat the grill. When it is hot put the dish carefully under it and grill, turning if necessary, to get it evenly browned. The top should look like a sheet of light brown glass and will be caramelized. Serve cold and crack the sugar top with a tap of the spoon before serving.

TRINITY HALL CIDER CUP

Mix together 4 tablespoons castor sugar, 2 bottles dry cider, 1 bottle Madeira, 150 ml ($\frac{1}{4}$ pint) each of brandy, rum shrub and sherry. Add a slice of dry toast sprinkled with grated nutmeg. Shrub is a home-made rum cordial made with lemon juice.

BLOATERS

The Scottish women were extremely deft and efficient at this work and the regional difference of the herring seasons, which is May and June in Scotland, meant that they were able to travel south to Yarmouth in September for the season there.

Great Yarmouth is now a holiday resort but was once a famous fishing town and port for the herring fleet. Many scenes in Dickens' David Copperfield are set in Great Yarmouth. Thomas Nashe, a contemporary of Shakespeare, wrote a poetical satire called Lenten Stuffe in 1599, about the town and the smoked herrings for which it is famous. Great Yarmouth has always had the reputation for producing the best bloaters which are herrings very lightly cured with salt and smoked. In this, they vary from the Red Herring which is well salted, so much so that it requires soaking in milk or water for a few hours before cooking in any way as for kippers, page 72.

BLOATERS

The best bloaters are still found on the east coast of England, particularly Great Yarmouth. They are very good grilled (see kippers page 72), served with butter and lemon or scrambled eggs.

BLOATER PASTE

An old-fashioned favourite for tea, in sandwiches or on toast.

Pour boiling water over 2 bloaters in a deep jug and leave for 10 minutes. Then drain, and, while warm, take out bones and skin. Then weigh fish. Mash or pound, either by hand or in a liquidizer, with an equal weight of butter. Add lemon juice or a few drops of tabasco sauce to taste. Season with freshly ground black pepper. You can either serve it now, with hot toast or in sandwiches, or you can put it into little pots and cover with clarified butter. It will keep in the refrigerator for about 3 days.

BLOATER FILLETS

Use fillets raw, cut into strips, or lightly cooked, mixed with cold sliced potatoes and some sliced beetroot. Dress with a little olive oil and lemon juice.

Yarmouth has first (O more than happy Port)
The honour to receive the King and Court
And entertain, season providing dishes
The King of England with the King of Fishes.

(Matthew Stevenson on Charles II's visit, 1671)

Scots women filling barrels of herrings, Great Yarmouth, Norfolk, 1912. Photographer, A. W. Yallop.

SAFFRON BUNS

These brewers are dressed in the traditional dress worn at the time. The Long Smock (Mr T. Shone); the Short Smock (Si Hills); the Fustian Jacket (Joseph Isabel). Essex was at one time well known for growing saffron, particularly at Saffron Walden which is a little over ten miles from Bishop's Stortford in Hertfordshire. This saffron was very popular in surrounding counties as well as in Essex and Saffron Buns were preferred at Easter time to Hot Cross Buns. Even as late as 1951 the local Essex paper reported they were still being eaten. Saffron growing was a great industry in Essex up until about 1800 when cheaper methods of production were found to deal with this finicky process, for something like 4,000 crocus flowers (Crocus sativus) are needed to make about 25 g (1 oz). This accounts, even today, for it being so expensive. It was also used as a medicine, i.e. saffron tea for curing measles, and a dye, as well as for culinary uses. Hakluyt said, in 1600, that a pilgrim from Asia Minor hid a corm in his staff and brought it to England. Those growing or gathering it were known as 'crockers'. The last field to produce this crocus was in Castle Street, under the shadow of the Norman castle in Saffron Walden.

Never buy powdered saffron for it can be adulterated, the orange-red strands give the best flavour. Saffron cake still survives in Cornwall and here Saffron is also used in bread and soups.

SAFFRON BUNS

3–4 g saffron, soaked in water	pinch of salt
450 g (1 lb) strong baker's flour	75 g (3 oz) butter

75 g (3 oz) currants	12 g ($\frac{1}{2}$ oz) fresh yeast, or 6 g
50 g (2 oz) candied peel, chopped	($\frac{1}{4}$ oz) dried
40 g (1$\frac{1}{2}$ oz) sugar	1 teaspoon sugar
	200 ml (7 fl oz) tepid milk

Soak the saffron in a little water overnight. Sift the flour and salt and rub in the butter. Add the currants, chopped peel and sugar, mixing well. Then make a well in the centre. Put the yeast and teaspoon of sugar with the tepid milk and let it work into a froth, then pour this, with the saffron water into the flour dough. Mix it up to make a softish dough, cover and leave in a warm place about 1 hour, or until double in size.

Grease a baking sheet, and pre-heat oven to 220°C, 425°F, Gas Mark 7. Turn out dough and knead a few minutes, shape into buns and put on sheet, spacing them out. Leave again to prove until they touch each other, then cook in pre-heated oven for about 12 minutes. Take out and brush with warm milk or egg and put back for 3 minutes. They were eaten hot for breakfast on Good Friday.

PEARS were baked with a few strands of saffron at Bedford Fair and known as 'wardens'. Warden pies were also made.

Smoking hot, piping hot,
Who knows what I've got
In my pot? Hot baked wardens.

Three brewers from Chelmsford Brewery Co., Wells and Perry, Duke Street, Chelmsford, Essex, c. 1864.

WARWICK PUDDING

Leicester Hospital was established by Robert Dudley, Earl of Leicester, by an act of incorporation obtained in 1571 for the reception of twelve poor men possessing not more than £5 a year, and a master. The first master, appointed by the Earl himself, was the famous Puritan, Thomas Cartwright. It is a very picturesque example of the half-timbered buildings that are a feature of Warwickshire.

WARWICK PUDDING

50 g (2 oz) glacé fruits, including ginger	650 ml (1¼ pints) milk
3 egg yolks	25 g (1 oz) gelatine
3 egg whites	3 tablespoons rum or brandy
100 g (4 oz) sugar	a little butter

Serves about 6

Butter a mould or a soufflé dish of about 1 litre (2 pint) size. Then decorate the bottom with the chopped glacé fruits.

Heat up the milk, and beat the egg yolks. When the milk boils, cool a little, then strain the egg yolks into it, whisking all the time. Add sugar. Dissolve the gelatine in a little warm water and stir until it is quite dissolved. Add to the custard.

Set aside to chill until it is beginning to set, like the consistency of raw egg white. Meanwhile whisk up the egg whites until very stiff. When the custard is ready, fold them in carefully so they get down to the bottom. Add the rum or brandy. Pour into the dish carefully, trying not to disturb the fruits. Chill to set. Turn out by wrapping a hot cloth around the dish, putting a serving plate on top and turning over quickly.

NUN'S BISKETS

These delicate little biscuits are almost as old as the building in the photograph.

175 g (6 oz) castor sugar	3 egg yolks and whites
100 g (4 oz) ground almonds	grated peel of 1 lemon and
100 g (4 oz) flour, sifted	1 teaspoon juice

Makes 24

Whisk the whites until stiff, then beat in almonds. Beat yolks well with the sugar and then mix the two mixtures very well. Add the flour, grated lemon rind and juice, folding in thoroughly.

Line a baking sheet with Bakewell paper or butter it well and drop large teaspoons of mixture on to it, well spaced apart. Sprinkle with castor sugar and cook in a pre-heated oven 170°C, 325°F, Gas Mark 3 for 20–30 minutes. Take off when cooked and cool on wire tray.

Lady sketching by Lord Leicester Hospital, Warwick, Warwickshire, c. 1900.

EEL STEW

Eels were a favourite food in Norfolk and also in many parts of London and eel-catchers, such as the man in the photograph, caught them by means of specially baited traps. It was a hard but good living at certain times of the year for eel pie, served cold, was a popular dish for high tea on Sunday. However, they were cooked many other ways, in soups, stews, fried, and particularly jellied and also smoked, in London. Eels are both nutritious and good to eat, but alas most of them today are exported to Holland and Germany.

EEL STEW

1 kg (2¼ lb) skinned and chopped eel	pepper and salt
	1 large onion, chopped
50 g (2 oz) butter	1 medium carrot, sliced
1½ litres (2½ pints) water	1 rounded tablespoon flour
1 tablespoon lemon juice	3 tablespoons double cream
1 tablespoon chopped parsley	*To garnish*
sprig of thyme and a bayleaf	chopped parsley
pinch of nutmeg	some fried-bread croûtons

Serves about 6

Soak the eel in salted water for about 15 minutes. The fishmonger will have skinned and chopped it for you if you ask him. Heat the butter and add the eel, then stew it for about 10 minutes but do not brown. Add the water, spices, herbs, onion and carrot, then season to taste. Boil, then reduce to a slow simmer for about 45 minutes. Cream the flour with the cream until smooth, and reserve.

Strain off the liquid into a clean saucepan. Pick out the eel and remove all the bones, then put the eel aside. Boil the strained eel liquor, then pour in a cupful of the flour and cream mixture, whisking well to avoid lumps. Pour this into the saucepan and stir all the time over heat until it thickens slightly, but do not boil. This should take about 5 minutes.

Taste for seasoning, put back the eel pieces and before serving add the fresh parsley. Serve with a bowl of croûtons.

Eel-catcher on the Norfolk Broads, late 1880s.

ROAST CHEESE

The velvet known as fustian was made in Birmingham but cut in Lymm. It was brought down there by canal. Some of the houses, still to be seen in Lymm, were very tall and the top floor (which was in one long room) was used to get the length. Each cutter was responsible for two frames and she walked up one frame cutting, then back again, cutting the other frame. The women started at 6 am in the morning and they could walk up to 16 miles a day. Fustian is a fabric in which the cloth face has more weft than warp threads, which are brushed into ribs of pile and cut as in corduroy, or cropped for velvet. The word is thought to come from the Arab el fustada describing a similar cloth. Chaucer refers to it as fustyan. Shakespeare calls it fustian.

Lymm is a charming village with a market cross standing on a sandstone dias and surmounted by a weathercock, with two stocks at the foot. The age of this cross has been a problem for experts to determine.

ROAST CHEESE

This is an old recipe from Lymm which was cooked in the oven, there being nothing else available at the time it was created. Today it can be made under a grill.

100 g (4 oz) Cheshire cheese, grated	100 g (4 oz) fresh breadcrumbs
2 egg yolks	100 g (4 oz) butter, soft
salt & pepper	4 slices bread, toasted one side only
2 teaspoons dry mustard powder	a little milk

Serves 4

Beat all dry ingredients in a mortar, then add the egg yolks and mix to a thick paste. If too thick to manipulate (as fresh Cheshire is difficult to obtain outside the county) add a little milk, but try not to. Spread this mixture thickly over the untoasted side of the bread and either grill slowly so that it cooks through, or put into a moderately hot (200°C, 400°F, Gas Mark 6) oven until cooked through and peaking golden.

CHESHIRE ALMOND BISCUITS

100 g (4 oz) butter	a few drops almond essence
100 g (4 oz) castor sugar	2 large eggs, beaten
100 g (4 oz) ground almonds	a little milk
175 g (6 oz) self-raising flour	25 g (1 oz) split almonds

Makes about 25

Cream the butter and sugar until very light. Add the beaten eggs gradually with a teaspoon of flour after each addition. Then add the remaining flour, the ground almonds and almond essence. If too thick add about 2 tablespoons milk until it is a pliable dough. Roll out on a lightly floured surface and cut either into rounds about 5 cm (2 in) across, or fingers. Put several split almonds on top and lay them on a greased baking sheet. Bake in a pre-heated oven at 190°C, 375°F, Gas Mark 5 for about 15–20 minutes, until a delicate gold. Lift off while hot and cool on a wire tray.

Women cutting the fustian (velvet), Lymm, Cheshire, c. 1890.

CHARLECOTE BISCUITS

The Shakespeare Memorial Theatre was opened on the poet's birthday, 23 April 1879, on land given by Charles Flower, who also gave £1,000 to launch a fund to build it. It was a gesture against many wealthy Warwickshire people who had done nothing previously to perpetuate the name of their famous son.

His wife's diary records her comments to him at the time: 'You have done it all . . . and if the theatre be used only once a year on 23 April it has been worth doing to honour Shakespeare on his own fête day in his native town.' It was destroyed by fire in 1926, but the library and picture gallery were saved. It was rebuilt in 1932.

William Shakespeare was born in Henley Street, which has been restored and contains many relics. Nash's House, where Shakespeare spent his retirement and where he wrote The Tempest, *still survives.*

CHARLECOTE BISCUITS

There is an interesting story about Shakespeare and these biscuits. It appears he was caught in the act of poaching deer at Charlecote Park and was punished for it. This began a life-long feud between Shakespeare and the Lucy family who owned the Park. The story goes that Shakespeare wrote a rude lampoon about Sir Thomas Lucy and nailed it on the gates of Charlecote House. In later years he is said to have based the character of Mr Justice Shallow on Sir Thomas Lucy. This recipe of the early 1800s, comes from Charlecote House and is taken from a little book called *Traditional Warwickshire Recipes* by Jo and Merlin Price.

225 g (8 oz) brown flour
175 g (6 oz) butter at room temperature

½ teaspoon baking powder
pinch of salt
4–5 tablespoons milk

Makes about 12

Pre-heat oven to 220°C, 425°F, Gas Mark 7. Lightly flour a baking sheet. Rub the warm butter into the flour until it resembles breadcrumbs. Add other dry ingredients and milk gradually to make a pliable but not sloppy dough. Turn out on to a lightly floured surface and roll out thinly. Cut into rounds the size of the top of a wine glass, put on to the sheet and bake for 5 minutes. Lift off when cooked and either eat hot with butter and honey (for which Warwickshire is well known) or serve cold with cheese.

The Shakespeare Memorial Theatre, Stratford-upon-Avon, Warwickshire, late 1870s.

BRANDY MOP CURLS

Ox roasting or the roasting of a whole pig is a traditional feature of the Mop Fair at Stratford-upon-Avon and other Warwickshire towns. It takes place at Michaelmas which is the end of September and it was a fair for hiring staff. In Stratford-upon-Avon it always took place opposite the Garrick Inn. Mop Fair, which still continues, is one of many fairs in this part of the country. In June there are Cherry Fairs and in Trinity Week on the Friday, there is the Lady Godiva procession in Coventry. Although the supposed ride of Earl Leofric's wife (Lady Godiva), without clothes, so that her husband would repeal the heavy taxes on Coventry people, took place in very early times, it was not established as a festival until the reign of Charles II. Coventry Godcakes are like Eccles cakes, page 155, but filled with mincemeat. They are three-cornered and a feature of that day, also for giving to godchildren.

J. Harvey Bloom in his book, Folklore, Old Customs and Superstitions in Shakespeare's Land, *1929, says that Mop Rock and Brandy Mop Curls were eaten on Mop Fair Day as well as the roast beef or roast pig.*

BRANDY MOP CURLS

These are similar to Brandy Snaps, a feature of some Yorkshire fairs and can be filled with cream or not, as desired.

100 g (4 oz) butter	2 rounded teaspoons ground
100 g (4 oz) golden syrup	ginger
100 g (4 oz) granulated sugar	1 teaspoon lemon juice
pinch of salt	1 tablespoon brandy
100 g (4 oz) flour	pinch of nutmeg

Makes about 25

Melt the butter, sugar and syrup in a saucepan. Then take from the heat and add the flour, salt, ginger, lemon juice and nutmeg. Finally, stir in the brandy. Stir very well off the heat, but see that it is still warm.

Spread baking sheets with Bakewell paper and put teaspoons of the mixture on it; about 6 teaspoons are enough, as the mixture will spread a great deal. Heat the oven to 160°C, 325°F, Gas Mark 3 and when hot put the trays in and bake for 8–10 minutes, or until they are golden brown, lacy and set.

Press these brandy snaps around the handle of a wooden spoon quickly, so they curl tightly. If they become difficult to roll, heat them in the oven slightly. When all are made, store in a tin which is airtight. Before serving stuff each end with a little whipped cream.

Golden syrup, which is a refined product, did not come in until the 1880s. Before that, black treacle was used.

Ox roasting at Mop Fair, Stratford-upon-Avon, Warwickshire, 1904.

WHOLEMEAL BREAD

Saunderson was one of the early makers of motorized farm machines which were extremely good for coping with the heavy Gault and Oxford clays. Bedford was also a centre for making straw hats.

WHOLEMEAL BREAD

This recipe makes excellent brown bread and this quantity makes 1 large loaf. See that all utensils and ingredients are warm before starting.

700 g (1½ lb) wholemeal flour
1 tablespoon lard or other fat
12 g (½ oz) dried yeast or
    25 g (1 oz) fresh
1 level teaspoon brown sugar

50 ml (2 fl oz) lukewarm water
generous 300 ml (½ pint) warm
    water
½ tablespoon black treacle
¼ teaspoon salt

Grease and warm a loaf tin about 25.5 × 10 cm (10 × 4 in) and pre-heat oven to 220°C, 425°F, Gas Mark 7.

Rub the fat into the warmed flour, then dissolve the yeast and sugar in the 50 ml (2 fl oz) tepid water and allow it to froth up. Add the yeast mixture to flour and mix the dough with more water in which the treacle and salt have been dissolved. Add a very little more warm water if the dough seems too stiff, but do not make it sloppy. Knead for 5 minutes, then put it into the prepared loaf tin, cut 3 nicks across the top, cover with a cloth and leave in a warm place for about 1 hour, or until dough has almost doubled in size.

When this has happened, put the loaf in the pre-heated oven for 10 minutes then reduce heat to 200°C, 400°F, Gas Mark 6 for another 30–35 minutes.

Turn out and cool on a wire tray. The loaf will sound hollow when cooked if tapped on the bottom. Ingredients can be doubled to make 2 loaves and they freeze very well.

Harvesting by a tractor-drawn reaper and binder turning the corner of a field, 1907.

PORK OR LAMB, STUFFED AND COOKED IN CIDER

This travelling press went round many villages in Worcester/Herefordshire and Shropshire. Anywhere, in fact, within reasonable distance where there was a plenitude of apples. The cider made in these parts is still excellent, dry and full of flavour, but alas the travelling apple press has gone.

Cider is extremely useful in the kitchen, as a marinade for meats, poultry or game and for cooking. In Normandy, France, it forms the basis of à la Normande *dishes.*

PORK OR LAMB, STUFFED AND COOKED IN CIDER

This makes either meat cooked this way quite delicious.

2 kg (4½ lb) loin of pork or lamb, boned
juice and peel of 1 lemon
450 g (1 lb) cooking apples, peeled and sliced
2 tablespoons brown sugar

a pinch of ground cloves
2 level teaspoons ginger
salt and pepper
2 tablespoons butter or oil
600 ml (1 pint) dry cider or apple juice

Serves about 8

Rub the meat inside and out with the lemon juice and sprinkle the peel inside. Then, laying the meat flat, slice the apples inside the meat, sprinkle with sugar, dot with the cloves and roll up, skewering or tying with string securely.

Rub all over the outside with a mixture of the ginger, salt, pepper, then brush over the oil or melted butter. Pre-heat the oven to 200°C, 400°F, Gas Mark 6. Put the meat into a roasting tin and cook in the pre-heated oven for 30 minutes, then pour off the fat, leaving the pan juices. Warm up the cider and baste with it every 20 minutes, finally, in the last half an hour, pouring over any that remains, still hot.

When cooked, put the meat on to a warmed dish and keep warm, then pour off any excess fat, reduce the gravy over a hot flame and serve separately. If a thicker gravy is liked then thicken with a little creamed flour.

If cooking pork you will not need apple sauce. Also, to make the crackling crisp, 10 minutes or so before it is ready, sprinkle with a few drops of cold water and then with salt.

SAMPSON

A favourite Cornish drink and cold cure.

Beat 2 eggs with 2 tablespoons of sugar, or to taste, then pour over, quickly, 1.1 litres (2 pints) hot cider and stir very briskly. Drink as hot as possible.

Travelling Cider Press, Worcester/Herefordshire, c. 1900.

VEAL CAKE

'*I was born nearly forty-four years ago, in Eastwood, a mining village of some three thousand souls about eight miles from Nottingham, and one mile from the small stream, the Erewash, which divides Nottingham from Derbyshire . . . the mines were, in a sense, an accident in the landscape, and Robin Hood and his merry men were not very far away.*' (*D. H. Lawrence writing in* Selected Essays, *1929.*)

'*The dwelling-room, the kitchen, was at the back of the house, facing inward between the blocks, looking at a scrubby back garden, and then at the ash-pits. And between the rows, between the long line of ash-pits, went the alley, where the children played and the women gossiped and the men smoked . . .*' (*Sons and Lovers, Chapter 1.*)

VEAL CAKE

Traditional Nottingham fare made from veal knuckles and set in a jelly.

2 meaty veal knuckles or 450 g (1 lb) pie veal	1 tablespoon parsley
salt and pepper	2 hard boiled eggs

serves about 4

Chop up the pie veal, put into a saucepan and cover with cold water. Bring to the boil, then season and simmer until the meat is very tender and the liquid reduced by about half. Lift out the meat, trim it of bone or gristle and shred or chop it finely. Let the strained liquor set in a bowl until cold and remove any fat.

Hard boil the eggs for 10 minutes in boiling water, then run under the cold tap, shell and reserve. Put the shredded meat, mixed with chopped parsley, in a mould or deep pudding basin, tucking the eggs in so that they are covered up. Then warm the liquid (which will be jellied), taste for seasoning and pour over to cover completely. Leave in a cold place to set, then turn out and serve cut in slices with a salad.

If available a little, 175 g (6 oz), finely chopped cooked ham or bacon can be added to the meat.

NOTTINGHAM FAGGOTS

There are many varieties of these all over the country: formerly pig's fry was used.

700 g (1½ lb) pig's liver	pinch of nutmeg, salt & pepper
225 g (8 oz) streaky pork (belly)	225 g (8 oz) white breadcrumbs
1 large onion, chopped	½ teaspoon each: dried sage & mixed herbs
2 small eggs	approx. 150 ml (¼ pint) stock
caul fat (which is the lacy fat from inside the pig). Most butchers can supply it.	

Enough for 6

Boil the meats with the onion until tender then mince it all. Combine with all the other ingredients and mix well. Either roll into balls and wrap in caul, or press it all into a baking tin, cover with caul, then mark into squares and bake at 190°C, 375°F, Gas Mark 5 for 1 hour and serve with vegetables and gravy.

Ascending in pit cage at Clifton Colliery, Nottingham, 1896.

STAFFORDSHIRE BREADED CHICKEN

Josiah Wedgwood was born at Burslem, Staffordshire in 1730 and already at least three generations of the family had been potters when it was little more than an ill-paid peasant craft. After his apprenticeship he was taken into partnership in 1754 by Thomas Whieldon of Fenton, the greatest English potter of his time. In 1759 Josiah went into business on his own account, founding the Wedgwood firm in Burslem, making the original creamware finished with a clear green glaze. He put fine earthenware within the reach of all but the very poorest class, the original cream pottery, now the Queen's Ware, increasing in popularity all over the world. His daughter became the mother of Charles Darwin FRS, author of The Origin of Species. *There were, of course, many other Staffordshire potters at this time. In 1764 he developed a fine-grained black basalt, smooth, richer in hue, used for relief plaques, busts, medallions, cameos as well as vases and tableware. It is still one of the firm's most popular products. Etruria had been the world's most up-to-date factory in the 18th century but subsidence made it unsuitable for modern development. Pottery production came to an end at the old Etruria works in June 1950 and a new fine modern works was built. Since 1966 there has been considerable growth of the Wedgwood group, both internally and by its acquisition of several other leading pottery companies.*

STAFFORDSHIRE BREADED CHICKEN

I first had this delicious roast chicken some years ago in Staffordshire, very near the Wedgwood Potteries, and I always think of it as connected with them.

1 roasting chicken about 1.8 kg (4 lb)
100 g (4 oz) butter
175 g (6 oz) fresh breadcrumbs
salt and milled pepper
1 egg, separated
finely grated rind 1 lemon
pinch each: cinnamon & nutmeg
1 tablespoon mixed: tarragon, parsley & lemon thyme

Serves 4–6

Stuffing
100 g (4 oz) fresh breadcrumbs
chopped herbs, 1 tablespoon
1 celery stick, chopped
2 streaky rashers, chopped
½ lemon rind grated
1 small onion, finely chopped
1 small egg
salt & pepper

Mix up all the stuffing ingredients and stuff the bird, securing firmly. Rub 50 g (2 oz) butter all over and cook in a pre-heated oven at 220°C, 400°F, Gas Mark 6 for 35 minutes. Meanwhile melt rest of butter, season breadcrumbs and stir yolk in. After 35 minutes spoon half melted butter over bird, then sprinkle on egged breadcrumbs. Put back for another 30 minutes. Then add grated lemon, spices and herbs to remaining crumbs with the whisked egg white, take out chicken and spread this mixture over too, and rest of the butter. Cook for a further 30 minutes or until crispy and golden brown.

Mr Sam Swann modelling heads in black basalt ware, Wedgwood Works, Etruria, Stoke-on-Trent, Staffordshire, 1898.

SPICE LOAF

The traditional festival of the Whalton Baal is held each year on old Midsummer's Eve, July 4. The alteration of the calendar in 1752 resulted in the date being moved forward by eleven days. Country folk round about, however, went on celebrating the festival at the old time.

A great bonfire is lit on the village green, there are Morris Dancers, sword dancing, and other dances; also fiddlers and the Northumbrian pipers. Cattle used to be driven through the fire to purify them and at one time the villagers themselves leapt through the flames. The festival still goes on, but the old habit of carrying burning branches around the village and fields to defend them from blight and witchcraft was recently discontinued.

Baal comes from the Anglo-Saxon bael, meaning a great fire.

SPICE LOAF

450 g (1 lb) self-raising flour	1 large egg
50 g (2 oz) lard	225 g (8 oz) sultanas
100 g (4 oz) margarine	100 g (4 oz) currants
100 g (4 oz) sugar	100 g (4 oz) raisins
1 level teaspoon mixed spice	50 g (2 oz) ground almonds
½ teaspoon ground nutmeg or mace	50 g (2 oz) glacé cherries
	50 g (2 oz) chopped mixed peel
300 ml (½ pint) milk and water, mixed	a few drops almond essence

Set oven at 170°C, 325°F, Gas Mark 3. Line the base of two 450 g (1 lb) loaf tins or one 900 g (2 lb) tin.

Rub fats into the flour, then add dry ingredients and mix well. Add fruit and essence and mix again. Beat egg with the milk and water and gradually add to the mixture until a soft, dropping consistency is obtained.

Pour into tin(s) and cook in pre-heated oven for 30 minutes, then lower to 150°C, 300°F, Gas Mark 2 for 1–1¼ hours. Cool on a wire tray and remove paper.

This spice loaf keeps very well in an airtight tin, or freezes well.

Whalton Baal Fire Ceremony, Whalton, Northumberland, 1903.

BEEF IN ALE

In the days before the turn of the century when annual holidays were unknown for workers, many Birmingham families came down to Hereford and Worcester for paid work in the open-air. It gave the children and their parents a change from over-crowded slum life and they enjoyed the comradeship which went with it.

On the last day of the hop-picking some pickers would chase the foreman and throw him in the big hop crib, then cover him with hop bines before tipping him out. This was known as 'cribbing' and thought to be an example of a sacrificial fertility rite. There was also a Hop-pickers' Fair before they left for home.

Cooking arrangements were primitive and stews which could be cooked over a wood fire were popular. A celebration dinner could be something like the following.

BEEF IN ALE

1.4 kg (3 lb) stewing steak, cubed
3 level tablespoons flour
2 level tablepoons beef dripping or oil
700 g (1½ lb) onions, chopped
900 ml (1½ pints) water or beef stock from bones

450 ml (¾ pint) brown ale or stout
pinch of mixed herbs
1 level teaspoon mustard powder
1 tablespoon Worcestershire sauce
salt and pepper

Serves 6–8

Trim the meat and then cube to convenient pieces. Sprinkle with half the flour, seasoned and also mixed with the mustard powder. Heat the dripping or oil and quickly fry the meat until brown all over. Put into a thick saucepan, then fry the onions until soft, but not brown. Add them to the meat. Add the water or stock and bring to the boil, then simmer gently. Skim off any scum, then add the herbs and keep simmering, covered.

Mix the remaining flour with a little of the brown ale or stout until it is smooth. Gradually stir in a little of the hot liquid, then tip it onto the meat and add the remaining ale. Bring back to a simmer and keep cooking for about 2½ hours or until tender. Finally add the Worcestershire sauce and stir well, then taste for seasoning.

Note: peeled potatoes can be added during the last 30 minutes, or dumplings.

DUMPLINGS are made by mixing 175 g (6 oz) flour with a pinch of salt, 75 g (3 oz) shredded suet, salt and pepper. Then add enough water, about 3–4 tablespoons to make a stiff dough. With floured hands, roll into about 15 small balls then either cook on top of the stew or boil in salted water for about 20 minutes, or until they float to the top, are risen and cooked through.

Families of hop-pickers relaxing, Bromyard, Worcestershire, c. 1890.

CAMBRIDGE SAUSAGES

Cambridgeshire was famous for many foods, such as choice asparagus from the Ely area, strawberries and also sausages. Many of the colleges also have their specialities, see page 23.

Cambridgeshire of all England
The Shire for men who understand
(Rupert Brooke)

CAMBRIDGE SAUSAGES

900 g (2 lb) lean pork, finely minced	1 level teaspoon dried sage
450 g (1 lb) shredded beef suet	½ teaspoon dried thyme & marjoram
50 g (2 oz) white breadcrumbs	salt and pepper
½ teaspoon grated nutmeg	1 large egg, beaten
grated rind of ½ lemon	

Makes about 16–20

Mix all ingredients together well and add the egg to bind and make a smooth paste. If possible, fill into sausage skins and leave in links. These are then boiled in salted water for 15–20 minutes and served with fried onions. However, if skins are not available then roll the sausage shapes in flour and fry in oil or butter.

GINGER PUMPKIN PIE

There are many orchards in Soham Mere in Cambridgeshire, and the Pumpkin Fair at Soham dates back to the Middle Ages.

225 g (8 oz) shortcrust pastry	50 g (2 oz) brown sugar
2 large eggs	300 ml (½ pint) single cream
1 level teaspoon ground ginger	225 g (8 oz) cooked pumpkin purée
¼ teaspoon mixed spice & cloves	

Line a 20 cm (8 in) fluted flan case with the pastry and lightly prick the bottom. Beat the eggs and whisk in the spices, brown sugar and the cream. Add the pumpkin purée and pour into the flan case.

Pre-heat the oven to 190°C, 375°F, Gas Mark 5. When hot, put the pumpkin pie in the centre of the oven and cook for 30–40 minutes until the filling is set and the top a gentle gold colour. Serve warm, with or without a little whipped cream.

Cambridge woman selling sausages in the market, 1901.

SALT BEEF OR PORK WITH PEASE PUDDING

Salt has been mined and prepared from the Northwich, Cheshire area since Roman times. However, rock salt was first discovered there by John Jackson of Halton, while prospecting for coal. Not very much is known about the early rock pits, but further exploration in Northwich found a lower bed there in 1781. In this area mining was continuous and important from 1791 to 1928. Some Cheshire mines are still operating making natural culinary salt of many varieties, the sole manufacturers being Ingram Thompson & Son Ltd, Lion Salt Works, Marston, Northwich, Cheshire, who sell to many well-known stores, in London and elsewhere. Cheshire salts are made by slowly evaporating Cheshire brine, using the open-pan process and all are free from chemical and artificial additives.

Salt mining was considered by contemporaries as quite a healthy job. The rock salt mines were dry, with good head room and a reasonable, even temperature all year round. There was no gas or sudden roof falls as in the coal mines. Constant pumping with fresh water, however, caused collapses which led to the demise of the mine in Northwich, but others in the area still continue.

The suffix 'wich' in many English place names denotes the presence of salt, i.e. Droitwich and others which might have marshy, salty land. All through the ages salt was a valuable commodity for preserving food and for horse and cattle licks. It has played a large part in English culinary tradition. True Cheshire cheese is said to acquire its particular flavour from the peculiarly saline quality of the mineralogy of Cheshire grazings. It has been made there for 300 years.

SALT BEEF OR PORK WITH PEASE PUDDING

Salting the meat
Rub a 1.5 kg (3½ lb) joint with coarse cooking salt to a thickness of about 3 cm (⅛ in), then rub in a little brown sugar and 25 g (1 oz) saltpetre. Put this in an earthenware or glass bowl and turn each day. If salting a very large joint it is easier to add a cupful of water so it becomes a liquid brine. Leave for about 1 week, but soak overnight before cooking. Serves 4–6.

To cook: put the soaked meat into a large saucepan with plenty of root vegetables, a sprig of thyme and parsley, barely cover with water and simmer for 20 minutes to the pound.

Pease Pudding is often served with it. Soak 450 g (1 lb) split peas overnight, then add a chopped onion and a dice of bacon. Tie loosely in a floured cloth (or cook separately well covered in water), put in with the meat and cook for about 1½ hours. Take out when cooked and mash up with a little butter, some seasonings, 1 egg and a few drops of Worcestershire sauce. Mix well and serve.

Working in the salt mines, Northwich, Cheshire, c. 1890.

SUSSEX POND PUDDING

Hastings is one of the Cinque Ports by virtue of the Norman castle started by William I and finished by the Count of Eu to protect the ancient harbour. It is both impressive and picturesque; many flint instruments have been found there which suggest an early and extensive neolithic population.

Hastings has for long been famous for the red and grey gurnard or gurnet found there, the red being the finer, which are fried, grilled or baked. However, one of the most excellent of all boiled puddings also comes from Sussex.

SUSSEX POND PUDDING

So called because when opened a pond of delicious juices run out.

225 g (8 oz) self-raising flour
100 g (4 oz) shredded or freshly
    chopped suet
approx. 150 ml (¼ pint) mixed
    milk and water

Filling
200 g (7 oz) warm unsalted
    butter
200 g (7 oz) soft brown or castor
    sugar
1 large lemon

Serves 4–6

Well butter a 1½ litre (2½ pint) pudding basin. First make the suet dough by mixing the flour and suet together. Add the milk and water slowly, mixing well until the dough is soft, but not too soft to roll. Put on to a lightly floured surface and knead slightly, then cut about a quarter off for the lid. Roll the rest into a circle and line the basin sides and bottom with this, making sure there are no gaps. Dampen any edges to make a good join.

Wash the lemon, dry it well and prick it all over with a thin sharp fork or small skewer. Pack the centre of the lined pudding basin with half the butter and sugar leaving a well in the middle, but not right down to the bottom. Place the lemon on to the butter/sugar mixture, then cover it with the remainder, using all the 200 g (7 oz) of butter and sugar.

Roll out the pastry to make the lid, dampen the edges slightly and press it on. Cover with either greased greaseproof paper or foil, double, with a pleat down the centre for expansion, and tie in place with string. If preferred use the old-fashioned method of a floured cloth, tied down, the corners tied at the middle which gives a handle. Steam over boiling water, or boil with the water half-way up for 3–4 hours. Turn out gently to serve and make sure everyone gets a small piece of the lemon.

An afternoon out at Hastings Castle, Sussex, 1867.

ORANGE CAKE

Aldeburgh is on the sea, a very attractive place, which had an important harbour in medieval times, and now an annual music festival is held there.

ORANGE CAKE

150 g (5 oz) butter, room temperature	150 g (5 oz) flour, sifted
150 g (5 oz) castor sugar	finely grated rind of 1 orange
2 eggs, large	1 level teaspoon baking powder

Pre-heat the oven to 180°C, 350°F, Gas Mark 4. Base line a 18–20 cm (7–8 in) tin and grease it.

Cream the soft butter and sugar until very light and fluffy. Gradually add the eggs and the orange rind. Mix in flour slowly, by degrees, and finally add the baking powder. If it is a little stiff add about 2 tablespoons milk but do not make it sloppy. Spoon into the prepared tin and bake in the centre of the oven for 1 hour, but test before taking out. Cool on a rack when ready.

Note: Lemon can be used instead of orange if preferred and the cake can be iced in the following way: sift 225 g (8 oz) icing sugar into a warm bowl, add the strained juice of 1 orange and beat well. Then if too stiff add a teaspoon or so of hot water. Pour over cake and allow to drip down sides or smooth with a spatula.

TREACLE TART

175 g (6 oz) shortcrust pastry (page 76)
For the filling

5 rounded tablespoons golden syrup	milk or egg to glaze
	rind of ½ large lemon, grated
4 heaped tablespoons fresh white breadcrumbs	1 tablespoon lemon juice

Serves 4–6

Roll out pastry on a lightly floured surface to a circle slightly larger than an 18–20 cm (7–8 in) flan or tart tin. Line it and put into a cool place while making the filling. Roll pastry trimmings into a ball and reserve.

Warm the syrup until thin and runny, but not boiling. Stir in breadcrumbs and leave to stand for about 10 minutes to absorb. Then check and, if too stodgy looking, add a little more warmed syrup. Stir in grated lemon rind and juice and spread mixture over pastry case, leaving the rim free. Roll out pastry ball to make strips for a criss-cross lattice. Brush pastry with milk or egg.

Put just above centre in a 190°C, 375°F, Gas Mark 5 heated oven and bake for 15 minutes. Lower to 180°C, 350°F, Gas Mark 4 and cook for a further 15 minutes or until golden and cooked.

Instruction in the kitchen, Thorpeness, near Aldeburgh, Suffolk, 1891.

CHOCOLATE CAKE

Birmingham is the second largest city in England and since about the end of the 19th century traditionally the home of small industries, although originally around St Paul's church it was known for silverware. Birmingham is said to have more canals than Venice, but many of them today are neglected and overgrown, although some have been restored to life.

The Bull Ring is still a great centre symbolized by the Rotunda, a shopping centre and the Central Library, with many other buildings and a complicated exchange of roads. It is the home of a fine symphony orchestra and has good art galleries. On the outer fringe are the works of the chocolate makers, Cadbury's, set in the garden suburb of Bournville.

CHOCOLATE CAKE

175 g (6 oz) butter or margarine, at room temperature
175 g (6 oz) castor sugar
2 eggs, large
175 g (6 oz) clear honey
50 g (2 oz) ground almonds

175 g (6 oz) plain flour, sifted with 65 g (2½ oz) cocoa
½ level teaspoon bicarbonate soda blended with 175 ml (6 fl oz) milk

Pre-heat oven to 150°C, 300°F, Gas Mark 2 and grease and base line a 20 cm (8 in) round cake tin. Put all cake ingredients into a large bowl and beat for 2–3 minutes with a wooden spoon. Pour into the prepared tin and bake in the pre-heated oven for 1¾–2 hours. Test before taking out, then turn out and cool on a wire rack. When cold, peel off paper, then cut the cake horizontally into two equal halves.

The Bull Ring, Birmingham, was Warwickshire, now West Midlands, c. 1895.

ICING AND FILLING

75 g (3 oz) butter
4 tablespoons milk or rum or brandy

1 rounded tablespoon cocoa, sifted
350 g (12 oz) icing sugar, sifted

Put butter, milk or spirit, and cocoa into a bowl and stir over a low heat until the butter has melted, but do not let it boil. Cool a little before adding the sifted icing sugar into this mixture and beating until quite smooth. Leave to get quite cold before using.

Sandwich the cake halves together with half the icing, then cover the top with the remainder and swirl it up with a fork. Dust with a little icing sugar before serving.

MUSHROOM PUDDING

This is an old Birmingham recipe to serve with roast beef.

Line a greased basin with suet crust (225 g (8 oz) flour, 100 g (4 oz) suet, a little water) keeping back a little for the lid. Then fill up with chopped field mushrooms, 50 g (2 oz) chopped ham or bacon, pepper, salt and two-thirds of the basin of stock or water. Cover with remaining crust, tie down with foil and steam for 2–2½ hours. Serves 4.

WILTSHIRE PICKLE FOR BACON AND HAM

Stonehenge comes from the Saxon word Stanhengist *meaning 'hanging stones'. It is one of the wonders and mysteries of Britain. This prehistoric monument has in turn been described as a Bronze Age temple or palace; an observatory for the Druids or as a headquarters for the numerous herding and farming communities which existed many years ago on Salisbury Plain. It was thought to have been started about 1850 BC and added to in 1500 to 1000 BC. Sir Edward Antrobus, a prominent Wiltshire land-owner, gained legal title to it in 1905 but the family subsequently sold it to the government. There is a similar construction nearby at Avebury, about the same period, but smaller.*

Wiltshire ham and bacon is mild-cured and delicious.

WILTSHIRE PICKLE FOR BACON AND HAM

The salt brine made from 700 g (1½ lb) salt has a little saltpetre added, also some juniper berries, 900 g (2 lb) black treacle, pepper-corns and 2.3 litres (2 quarts) beer all boiled. When the liquid is cool, the meat is added and left in for about 3 weeks. It must be turned daily and the pickle rubbed well in. Then it is dried before storing and soaked overnight before cooking.

HAM BAKED WITH CHESTNUTS

Bone a 1.8–2.3 kg (4–5 lb) ham and soak it. Cover with water or cider and simmer for 25 minutes to the pound. Strip off the skin when cool enough.

450 g (1 lb) chestnuts, either fresh or canned, without sugar	50 g (2 oz) butter or 2 tablespoons cream
2 tablespoons brown sugar	3 tablespoons breadcrumbs pepper

Serves about 10–12

Mash the chestnuts well, add the sugar and either half the butter or cream and some pepper. Lay the ham on a board and stuff the cavity with as much of this as it will hold, then press together and secure. Put into an ovenproof dish.

Make a criss-cross pattern with a sharp knife on the top of the ham. Mix the breadcrumbs into the rest of the chestnut mixture and press this over the top. Add about 300 ml (½ pint) or so of the ham stock around the dish and put into a pre-heated oven at 200°C, 400°F, Gas Mark 6 for about ½ hour or until the top is crisp.

Yeomanry Cavalry Officers at Stonehenge, Salisbury Plain, Wiltshire, 1860.

RABBIT AND BACON STEW

The farm labourer's name was Charles Sweeting who was born in East Anglia in 1826 and worked all his life on the land until he retired to an almshouse with his sister. He died in 1913.

RABBIT AND BACON STEW

A favourite dish with all country people and also with me. Once cooked, the rabbit can be taken from the bone and put with the chopped bacon into a pie dish and covered with a pastry crust. It is delicious and will be jellied when cold.

1 rabbit 1.1–1.5 kg (2½–3 lb), jointed & rolled in flour
450 g (1 lb) boiling bacon in one piece, collar or shoulder, soaked
2 large onions, sliced

450 g (1 lb) carrots
225 g (8 oz) white turnips, sliced
600 ml (1 pint) stock
sprig of thyme
2 tablespoons parsley, chopped
salt and freshly ground pepper

Serves 6

Soak the piece of bacon overnight or for at least 4 hours. Take out and simmer in fresh, cold water for about 45 minutes until it is cooked enough to strip the skin from the top and chop into large cubes. The rabbit, which has been jointed, can also soak in salted water for a few hours, then take out, dry, roll in seasoned flour and put the two meats into a large saucepan with the chopped onions and carrots, thyme, salt and pepper and the stock. Make up with water to barely cover the meats. Boil, then simmer for about 1 hour, add the chopped turnips and half the parsley. Bring back to the boil and simmer again for 30–40 minutes or until the rabbit is tender. If a thicker gravy is liked, blend 1 tablespoon flour with cold water, add a little of the hot stock, stir until smooth, then pour into the saucepan stirring continuously. Garnish with the remaining parsley before serving, and taste for seasoning. Dumplings (see page 48) can be added, if liked, for the last 30 minutes.

RHUBARB WINE

When I lived in Hertfordshire, Ellen Howe, who worked for me for years, often made this delicious wine. Here is her recipe as told to me: 'Wipe and cut up 2.3 litres (2 quarts) of rhubarb and put in a pan with 2 lemons and 2 tablespoons of dried hops (Champagne rhubarb makes the best wine). Pour 1 gallon (4.5 litres) boiling water on it and let it stand for 9 days, then strain through a cloth. Put 1.8 kg (4 lb) sugar into the pan and add 1.1 litres (1 quart) boiling water and stir well until sugar is dissolved. Bottle it and let it ferment for about 4 days. After it has done fermenting, cork down and let it store in a cool, dark place. It can be drunk after 2 months, but the longer it is kept, the better it becomes.'

East Anglian farm worker resting from sickle cutting, enjoying his bread and cheese, c. 1880s.

GAMMON AND SPINACH

The Dunmow Flitch Trial has a very long history. It is said to date back to the 12th century when Lady Juga, sister of Ralph Baynard, Lord of the Manor at the Domesday Survey, offered a flitch, which is an entire side of bacon, to any couple who were willing to swear that they had lived for a year and a day without a single quarrel and desired no other. Chaucer mentions it in The Miller's Tale, in the Prologue to The Tale of the Wife of Bath.

> The bacoun was not fet for hem I trowe,
> That som men han in Essex at Dunmowe.

There is a judge and a mock jury of six local maidens and six batchelors before which two couples have to swear the following oath:

> You doe swear by custom of confession
> That you ne're made Nuptiall Transgression,
> Nor since you were married man and wife,
> By household brawls or contentious strife
> Or otherwise in bed or at boarde,
> Offended each other in Deed or in Word
> Or in a twelve moneths time and a day
> Repented not in thought in any way
> Or since the Church Clerke said Amen
> Wish't yourselves unmarried agen,
> But continue true and in desire,
> As when you joyn'd hands in Holy Quire.

GAMMON AND SPINACH

Gammon of bacon is the best cut from the top of the hind leg. Sometimes the whole leg or gammon is boiled or baked, but in these days of smaller families it is the thickly cut slices which are more popular.

1 kg (2¼ lb) fresh spinach, picked over and washed
pepper and salt
pinch of nutmeg

3–4 tablespoons double cream
two 350 g (12 oz) gammon steaks
a little melted butter

Enough for 2

First cook the drained spinach with just the water on the leaves from the last wash. Cook for about 10 minutes, until soft, turning once, then drain very well squeezing out any water. Chop or purée spinach, add seasonings and the cream, then keep hot. Brush the gammon steaks over with melted butter and grill on both sides. Serve on top of the creamed spinach.

Dunmow Flitch, trial of the claimants, Great Dunmow, Essex, 1890s.

GRASMERE GINGERBREAD

Herdwick sheep are a feature of the Lake District: their colour varies from dark grey to a dark chocolate brown, and they are extremely hardy, as well as being very attractive to look at. The wool is very dense, good for spinning, and another advantage is that they do not stray but stay on their own 'heaf'. Swaledale sheep are crossed with Herdwick, their wool fetching a higher price than the other, so consequently purebred Herdwick sheep are becoming rarer. Beatrix Potter the well-known writer of children's stories invested the income from her books in Lakeland sheep farms and was for many years chairman of the Herdwick Sheep Breeders Association.

GRASMERE GINGERBREAD

As made by an elderly lady called Mrs Beetham and distributed to the children who took part in the Ambleside Rushbearing Ceremony which takes place on the Sunday nearest to St Oswald's Day, 5 August. Six young girls in green-and-white tunics carry a hand-spun linen rush-sheet to commemorate the days when the damp earthen church floors were strewn with rushes. There is Maypole dancing as well.

Recipes gathered by Mrs Jean Seymour and kindly given to me.

175 g (6 oz) white sugar	450 g (1 lb) flour, sifted
100 g (4 oz) butter or margarine	2 teaspoons bicarbonate of soda
4 rounded tablespoons golden syrup	2 teaspoons baking powder
450 ml ($\frac{3}{4}$ pint) milk	6 level teaspoons ground ginger

Boy herding sheep and lambs, Lake District, c. 1900.

Melt sugar, butter, milk and syrup but do not boil. Add baking powder and bicarbonate of soda and stir very well off the heat. Pour on to sifted flour and ginger and heat. Pre-heat oven to 190°C, 375°F, Gas Mark 5. Pour mixture into a 20 cm (8 in) shallow tin and bake for 45–60 minutes, or until cooked and golden brown.

Mark into squares while still warm. When cool, turn out.

CUMBERLAND TOFFEE

This can also be made with black treacle (molasses). It is very good for toffee apples and this amount covers 18 small apples.

275 g (10 oz) sugar	100 ml (4 fl oz) water
100 g (4 oz) golden syrup	$\frac{1}{2}$ tablespoon butter
pinch of salt	

Melt all ingredients slowly in a heavy saucepan. Boil to 140°C, 280°F, 'small crack' on a sugar thermometer or until some dropped into cold water is brittle. Grease a shallow tray, about 6 mm ($\frac{1}{4}$ in) deep and pour into it. While still warm mark into squares. Leave to go cold, then break up into pieces.

COD AND MUSTARD SAUCE

Jeremiah Colman started with a flour mill in 1814 at Stoke Holy Cross, about four miles south of Norwich. An earlier owner, Mr Ames, had already started to make mustard, so when Mr Colman bought he had to choose whether to continue, which he did. His nephews set up as Colman Brothers in London and became agents for the goods of Jeremiah Colman in 1844. A move was made to Carrow in 1854 where the first of many large mustard mills was established and, in 1903, J. & J. Colman took over another mustard firm. This mill operated until the early 1950s when the present site in Norwich was commissioned.

Two strains of mustard have been cultivated by Colman's, known as Stoke and Kirby, after the two Norfolk villages in which the breeding work was carried out. The village of Trowse on the outermost fringe of the Colman's area has become 'colonized' by Colman's and to this day is largely inhabited by the firm's employees.

Although mustard and meat have made a happy marriage, it is also a part of many other dishes and sauces. It goes particularly well in a sauce with herrings or cod.

COD AND MUSTARD SAUCE

4 large cutlets or fillets of cod, weighing about 225 g (8 oz) each
1 lemon
salt and pepper
300 ml (½ pint) milk
50 g (2 oz) butter

Serves 4

For the sauce
1 tablespoon each: butter and flour
1 rounded teaspoon dry mustard powder
1 level teaspoon made mustard
300 ml (½ pint) fish stock
2 tablespoons cream
pepper

Butter an ovenproof dish and lay the fish in it. Season well and sprinkle with about 1 tablespoon lemon juice. Pour the milk round the fish and dot the tops with half the butter in small pieces. Pre-heat the oven to 180°C, 350°F, Gas Mark 4, cover the fish with foil and bake for about 30 minutes. When cooked, remove any bones or skin, drain off the liquid and reserve.

To make the sauce: heat the butter, stir in the mustard powder and flour, mix well and cook for 1 minute. Add the milky fish liquid making it up to half a pint. Stir all the time to avoid lumps and when it is smooth and creamy add the made mustard, still stirring. Just before serving, add the cream, heat up but do not reboil.

Melt the remaining butter from the fish ingredients and serve the fish with the butter poured over and the mustard sauce separately.

Packing Colman's mustard in pictorial tins for the Christmas trade, Norwich, Norfolk, c. 1880.

NEWCASTLE PUDDING

This is like a good bread and butter pudding and was very popular in the 'eighties and 'nineties.

NEWCASTLE PUDDING

6 small slices of crustless bread (brown, fruit, or white), buttered
50 g (2 oz) currants or raisins
1 tablespoon chopped candied peel

75 g (3 oz) brown sugar
grated rind 1 lemon
2 eggs
450 ml (¾ pint) milk
a little butter

Serves 4–6

Lightly butter an ovenproof dish and lay half the buttered bread slices on the bottom. Sprinkle with the dried fruit and peel, the sugar and lemon rind. Cover with the remaining bread slices, buttered side down.

Heat the milk to boiling, then take it off the heat. Beat the eggs lightly and quickly pour the milk over them, stirring all the time. Pour this all over the bread and leave to stand for about 30 minutes until most of it is absorbed.

Then heat the oven to 180°C, 350°F, Gas Mark 4, and when hot, cook the pudding in a pan containing water to half-way up for about 1 hour. Eat hot with a little brown sugar sprinkled over the top and some cream if you like.

It was also made in a basin, covered and steamed over boiling water for 1 hour.

The sands, Tynemouth, Tyne and Wear, 1888.

KIPPERS

Craster is a small fishing village in Northumberland famous for its oak-smoked kippers. L. Robson & Sons Ltd have had a factory there for over a hundred years where excellent herrings (from South Shields) are smoked by the traditional method over a fire of green oak chips. This gives the fish the best flavour in which no chemicals or colouring are used. The Robson curing house is open to view from June to September. Local fishermen also catch lobsters and crabs.

KIPPERS

Kippers make an excellent breakfast dish either grilled and served with a knob of butter and pepper, which is my favourite method, or jugged. This is simply done in the following way:

JUGGED KIPPERS

Put the kippers tails-up in a deep earthenware jug. Pour over enough boiling water to cover them and leave for 7–10 minutes. Drain them well and serve hot with buttered slices of brown bread.

BAKED KIPPERS

A good method for those without a grill or who dislike the smell of kippers cooking: sandwich a pair of kippers together with a good knob of butter in the middle. Wrap well in foil securing the ends and bake in a hot oven 220°C, 425°F, Gas Mark 7 for 10 minutes.

KIPPERS WITH SCRAMBLED EGGS

Cook the kippers whichever way you prefer and while they are cooking, melt a knob of butter in a non-stick saucepan. When hot, add 2 beaten eggs, seasoned. Stir all the time until they are creamy and still runny on top, then serve with the kippers either on toast, or not.

KIPPER PASTE

1 pair of Craster or undyed kippers	lemon juice
	a little cream, optional
butter	
cayenne pepper & pinch of mace	

You can use dyed kippers, but naturally the others are best. Cook them by the jugged method and after draining remove all skin and bones. Weigh flesh and add an equal amount of butter, the spices and lemon juice to taste. A little whisked cream or plain yoghurt can be added if liked, or well-mashed cottage cheese which makes the paste less rich. If pressed into a pot and sealed with clarified butter or foil, it will keep for a week. Serve with toast or dry water biscuits.

KIPPERS IN LEMON JUICE

Lay the kippers in a shallow dish which will take them without squashing. Pour over enough lemon juice to almost cover them and cover with foil. Leave for at least 8 hours (they can stay longer), turning over so that both sides are immersed. Take out, drain and slice thinly. They taste just like a coarse smoked salmon and are served the same way with brown bread and butter.

Packing kippers at Craster, Northumberland, c. 1910.

L UNCHEON CAKE

Hindhead is 800 feet up and one of the finest viewpoints in southern England, surrounded by woods and headlands.

Although the picnic now seems a particularly English habit, it originally progressed from France (piques-niques) and Germany (Picken und Nicken). About 1800 a society was formed in London known as 'The Pic Nic Society' which was, however, indoors and gave theatrical performances as well as concerts, but each person supplied a dish for the evening, for which lots were drawn and each person was obliged to take the food of the number he had drawn.

'A stick of horseradish, a bottle of mint sauce well corked, a bottle of salad dressing, a bottle of vinegar, made mustard, pepper, salt, good oil and pounded sugar. If it can be managed, take a little ice. It is scarcely necessary to say that plates, tumblers, wine-glasses, knives, forks, and spoons must not be forgotten; as also teacups and saucers, 3 or 4 teapots, some lump sugar, and milk, if this last-named article cannot be obtained in the neighbourhood. Take 3 corkscrews.' (Mrs Beeton, 1861)

LUNCHEON CAKE (also called PICNIC CAKE)

Luncheon cake was a regular cake in most households' week. It is a plainish cake with quite a lot of fruit in it, but no eggs. When stale, it was eaten spread with butter, or with cheese. It keeps very well in a tin.

175 g (6 oz) butter or dripping	175 g (6 oz) raisins and sultanas,
450 g (1 lb) flour	mixed
225 g (8 oz) soft brown or white	3 tablespoons malt vinegar
sugar	just over 150 ml (¼ pt) milk
225 g (8 oz) currants	1 teaspoon bicarbonate of soda

Rub the butter into the flour well, then add the sugar and the fruit. Put the vinegar into a deep jug, add the milk keeping back a spoonful or so. Warm this to tepid heat and mix with the bicarbonate of soda. Add this quickly to the jug taking care not to let it froth up and run over.

Pre-heat the oven to 180°C, 350°F, Gas Mark 4. Prepare an 18–20 cm (7–8 in) cake tin by lining it and greasing it slightly, then pour the mixture in, levelling off the top. Bake in the pre-heated oven for 20 minutes, then lower the heat to 160°C, 325°F, Gas Mark 3 for a further 40–50 minutes.

Turn out on to a wire tray, take off papers and cool. It is best to leave a day before cutting.

Picnic at Hindhead, Surrey, 1919.

YORKSHIRE CURD TARTS

Harrogate is a fashionable spa town which caters for all kinds of people. There are many attractions there, elegant shops, a good theatre, concerts, as well as the Pump Room which was built in 1913, where medicinal waters are taken. The Tewit Spring was first recognized c. 1570 by a member of the Slingby family who fenced and protected it. In the late 17th and 18th centuries John's Well was popular, so many hotels, boarding houses and shops were built around it, forming High Harrogate village.

YORKSHIRE CURD TARTS

These delicious tarts are eaten for tea all over Yorkshire and are extremely good either cold or hot.

For the pastry
225 g (8 oz) plain flour, sifted
100 g (4 oz) butter or margarine
1 tablespoon castor sugar
pinch of salt
1 egg yolk, beaten
1–2 tablespoons cold water

For the filling
225 g (8 oz) fresh curds or
    sieved cottage cheese
50 g (2 oz) castor sugar
1 teaspoon grated lemon rind
3 eggs, separated
50 g (2 oz) currants
2 tablespoons butter, melted
2 teaspoons rum, optional
grated nutmeg for sprinkling

Makes about 24 small tarts or 1 large one

First make the pastry and chill it for at least half an hour. Meanwhile put curds or sieved cottage cheese in a basin and add sugar, currants, egg yolks, lemon rind and melted butter. Also add the rum if using. Finally beat egg whites until stiff and add to the mixture.

Heat the oven to 180°C, 350°F, Gas Mark 4. Roll out pastry and cut to line either a 20 cm (8 in) flan tin or 24 small patty tins. Divide the filling between them and finally sprinkle with freshly grated nutmeg.

Bake in the pre-heated oven for 25–30 minutes or until the filling is set and firm. Serve warm or cold.

Winter Gardens, Harrogate, Yorkshire, 1920.

MELTON MOWBRAY PORK PIE

Stilton, known as 'the King of English Cheeses' was not first made at Stilton. In 1730 a Mrs Paulet of Wymondham (Leicestershire) made a cream cheese which she sent to a relation, Cooper Thornhill, who was landlord of The Bell Inn at Stilton. His customers were numerous as it was on a coaching route and they praised it highly, so it became known as Stilton cheese. Daniel Defoe in A Tour Through the Whole Island of Great Britain remarks: '... we passed Stilton, a town famous for cheese.' Other makers of early Stilton were a dairy maid at Quenby Hall in Leicestershire and Mrs Orton of Little Dalby. Stilton should be cut, not scooped. Red Leicester cheese is also delicious, known since the middle 18th century.

Melton Mowbray, Leicestershire, is also famous for Melton Mowbray Pork Pie and the Melton Hunt Rich Fruit Cake, taken with the stirrup cup by the hunt for over 100 years. Both these are still made at the shop in Melton Mowbray, where they have been made since 1851, by Dickinson and Morris.

MELTON MOWBRAY PORK PIE

From an original recipe given by Dickinson and Morris, who say it must have the bowed sides to be traditional. Makes a 450 g (1 lb) pie.

All pastry ingredients must be kept warm. Pre-heat oven to 220°C, 425°F, Gas Mark 7.

Stilton Rounds at Leicester Market, c. 1872.

bones from meat used for filling
2 pig's trotters
1 sliced carrot
1 medium onion
herbs

First make the jellied stock by putting the above into a saucepan and adding about 1.1 litres (2 pints) water. Boil, then simmer for 2–3 hours, cool and de-fat.

To make the hot water pastry	For the filling
225 g (8 oz) plain flour	450 g (1 lb) lean pork, finely
1 level teaspoon salt	chopped not minced
100 g (4 oz) lard	salt & pepper
65 ml (2½ fl oz) milk and water mixed	$\frac{1}{4}$ teaspoon dried sage
	2 tablespoons water or stock
beaten egg to glaze	$\frac{1}{4}$ teaspoon anchovy essence

Sift flour and salt into a warm bowl. Heat lard, milk and water until boiling, then add to the flour mixing with a wooden spoon. When cool enough knead by hand. It must be warm when raised. Reserve a quarter for the lid and leave covered, in warm place. Roll out remainder to 6 mm ($\frac{1}{4}$ in) thick and gently mould around a floured and greased jam jar. Leave to cool. Then put in filling, cover with lid, pressing down well, brush with the egg. Make a hole in the middle, bake in a pre-heated oven for 20 minutes, then lower to 180°C, 350°F, Gas Mark 4 for 1–1½ hours. When cooked, pour jelly stock through hole in the top and leave for 12–24 hours before cutting.

NORTHUMBERLAND BAKED HADDOCK WITH EGG SAUCE

In 1815 a broadsheet published a celebration ballad in Newcastle and all over Tyneside praising Wellington's victory at Waterloo. Part of it went as follows:

May the Trade of the Tyne the ocean abound
And Peace all her blessings bestow,
The pastures of Britain with Plenty be crowned
And strong be the milk of the cow.

The wooden ship of the line in the photograph could well have been around at the time of Waterloo.

NORTHUMBERLAND BAKED HADDOCK WITH EGG SAUCE

This haddock recipe is from the 1870s.

1 whole haddock about 1.4 kg
  (3 lb) in weight, cleaned
2 rounded tablespoons white
  breadcrumbs

1 level tablespoon shredded
  suet
1 shallot, minced
pinch of dried thyme

salt & black pepper and nutmeg
1 small egg
4 tablespoons salted water

For the sauce
2 eggs, hard-boiled for 10
  minutes
100 g (4 oz) butter, melted
sprigs of parsley

Serves 4

See the fish is well cleaned and pat it dry. Mix together the breadcrumbs, suet, shallot, thyme, salt, pepper and a pinch of nutmeg, then bind it all with a small beaten egg. Put this into the gullet of the fish and secure it well. In the old days the fish was then trussed in the shape of an S. Lay it in an ovenproof dish, pour the salted water around, cover with a lid or foil and bake at 180°C, 350°F, Gas Mark 4 for about 45 minutes or until the fish is cooked.

Meanwhile, hard boil the eggs, cool under cold water and shell. Then cut in half and remove the yolks. Mash these very well. Melt the butter but do not brown it, add the yolks mixing well, then chop up the whites and add them, then heat up. Dish up the fish, pour a little sauce over it and serve the rest separately. Garnish with a few sprigs of parsley.

Note: if preferred the stuffed fish can be wrapped in double foil and baked for the same time.

Shipping on the Tyne, Newcastle on Tyne, 1888, with paddle steam-tugs preparing to tow an old wooden ship of the line.

OYSTER CUTLETS

Ye Olde Barley Mow dates from 1561 and still continues as an excellent pub with good food. It is now a central point of the new Golden Square shopping complex in Warrington. The oyster bar at the right of the picture was formerly the Old Fox Inn, owned by Charlie Lee. He was renowned for writing poetic advice to his customers.

'Keep your soul pure, eat good oysters now, to a glass of good beer in the Old Barley Mow.'

Warrington first grew up around a river ford, now the Manchester Ship Canal. In 1848 it was the first town to have a public library supported by the rates.

OYSTER CUTLETS

When this recipe was evolved oysters were about six old pence per dozen so they were a valuable source of protein for the poor with a glass of ale. As Sam Weller said in *Pickwick Papers*: 'It's a wery remarkable circumstance, sir, that poverty and oysters always seem to go together.'

2 rounded tablespoons white
    breadcrumbs soaked in
    2 tablespoons cream
100 g (4 oz) cooked chicken,
    minced
salt and freshly ground white
    pepper

1 dozen oysters, fresh or
    canned, drained and chopped
2 egg yolks
egg, breadcrumbs & oil for
    coating

Serves 4

Soak the breadcrumbs in the cream until some has been absorbed. Then pound the chicken, finely chop the oysters and add seasoning. Bind with the beaten egg yolks. With floured hands shape into cutlets, dip into raw beaten egg, then into breadcrumbs. Heat some oil (about 2–3 tablespoons) and fry them on both sides until golden. Drain on paper and keep warm. Serve as a first, or savoury course.

CHESHIRE PORK AND APPLE PIE

175 g (6 oz) shortcrust pastry
1 kg (2 lb) lean, boned pork such
    as fillet
3 rashers unsmoked streaky
    bacon, chopped
1 large onion, finely sliced
salt, pepper & nutmeg

1 tablespoon brown sugar
375 g (12 oz) sweet eating apples
approx. 150 ml ($\frac{1}{4}$ pint) dry cider
    or light beer
25 g (1 oz) butter
a little milk for glazing pastry

Serves 4–6

First make the pastry (see page 95) and let it rest. Then trim the meat and de-rind the bacon, also prepare the apples and slice them. Take a deep pie dish and put layers of pork and seasoning, then the bacon and onion mixed and lay this on top. Put the sliced apples over the top, scatter the sugar over and finally dot with butter and pour over the cider or ale to barely cover. Cover with pastry, brush with milk to glaze and bake at 200°C, 400°F, Gas Mark 6 for 15–20 minutes, then lower to 160°C, 325°F, Gas Mark 3 for a further 45 minutes or until the meat seems tender when pressed with a thin skewer. Cover with greaseproof paper if it's getting too brown. Originally this had pastry top and bottom but I do not think it needs it. It can be eaten hot or cold.

Ye Olde Barley Mow with oyster stall and oyster bar at right of photograph, c. 1890s. Warrington, Cheshire (was Lancashire until 1974).

WELLINGBOROUGH HOUGH AND DOUGH

This was a commonplace scene all over Britain before the last war, and even today some of these country markets have re-opened, many of them now under cover, not in the open air as this one. There was usually a pub handy, as there is here on the right, so that some business could be concluded over a pint.

WELLINGBOROUGH HOUGH AND DOUGH

Serves about 3–4

This is the traditional dish all over Northampton. It consists of a suet dough, rolled out and used to line the sides only of a meat tin. A pork hock joint weighing about 700 g (1½ lb) is put in the middle and surrounded with sliced potatoes and onions. It is sprinkled with sage, salt and pepper, and hot stock to half-fill the tin, then covered with a lid (or foil). It is put into a pre-heated oven at 200°C, 400°F, Gas Mark 6 for about 20 minutes, then the heat is lowered to 180°C, 350°F, Gas Mark 4 and cooked for 1½ hours. The cover is removed for 30 minutes after that to let the top brown. It is very good cooked without the dough. Incidentally 'hough' is the same as 'hock'.

CASSEROLE OF SWEETBREADS

This recipe was given to me by an elderly lady from Northampton and is delicious.

450 g (1 lb) sweetbreads
225 g (8 oz) streaky bacon, de-rinded
2 medium onions, finely sliced
100 g (4 oz) button mushrooms
2 teaspoons chives, chopped
1 tablespoon parsley, chopped
salt and pepper
4 tablespoons cider or white wine
breadcrumbs

Serves 4

First soak the sweetbreads for 1 hour in tepid water. Drain and put in a pan with fresh water to cover, bring slowly to the boil and simmer for 7 minutes. Plunge the drained sweetbreads into cold water at once. When cool, skin them and take off any gristle and tissues.

Line a dish with some of the bacon rashers, then put the onions, mushrooms, herbs and sweetbreads on top. Season to taste and add cider or wine. Cover with the rest of the rashers. Lay foil over the top and bake at 180°C, 350°F, Gas Mark 4 for about 1 hour. Then take off the foil, sprinkle the top with breadcrumbs and put back in the oven until crisp and brown. Serve with a mushroom sauce.

Market day in Market Street, at Wellingborough, Northamptonshire, c. 1900.

REGENCY LAMB CHOPS

Brighton, from the time of the Domesday Book was called Bright-helmston because of a bright, white stone found on the shore which helmsmen used to steer their ships by. Up until the middle of the 18th century it was a small, far from elegant, fishing village. However, when a Dr Russell taught the medicinal value of sea-bathing, the future George IV brought the Court there to relax which made it a popular resort. He commissioned Henry Holland to build the Royal Pavilion there and it was completed and remodelled by John Nash in 1819 after the style of the Moghul palaces of India, as a monument to Britain's connections with the Far East. It was at this time that the town became known as Brighton. The Southdown lamb and mutton was a great delicacy and very much liked by the Prince Regent who had a large appetite.

REGENCY LAMB CHOPS

8 loin of lamb chops
8 rashers streaky bacon
40 g (1½ oz) butter
1 grated shallot or small onion
½ teaspoon finely chopped
  rosemary
salt and freshly ground black
  pepper
For the sauce
225 g (8 oz) picked over
  redcurrants
50 g (2 oz) sugar or to taste
5–6 tablespoons red wine

Serves 4

Take the bones from the chops making a *noisette* of the meat and remove centre fat. Soften the butter and add the grated shallot or onion, rosemary, salt and pepper and work it in well, then divide into 8 pats and chill. De-rind the bacon and lay the boned chop out flat and season with pepper.

Put a pat of the shallot butter in the centre and roll it into a circle, then wrap a rasher of bacon around it and secure with a thin skewer or cocktail stick. Have ready a pre-heated grill and grill the chops for about 7 minutes, on each side, but once they brown, lower the heat a little to let them cook.

Meanwhile, cook the topped redcurrants with the sugar and wine for about 10 minutes, until they are soft. Alternatively, they can be liquidized or put through a vegetable mill if preferred. Serve around the chops.

Brighton Beach, Sussex, c. 1880.

TATIE CAKE

Durham was occupied by the Romans. Founded by Ida in 574AD, it ceased to exist as a separate kingdom in 792 when the last of the Heptarchy came under the rule of Egbert. In 685 Edfrid, King of Northumbria made a grant of all country between Wear and Tyne to Cuthbert, the northern apostle. Northumbria was converted to Christianity before the middle of the 7th century. When Cuthbert died, his body did not decompose after ten years, so the monks who were looking after it wandered with it in a coffin for many years, hiding the body from Danish raiders. Eventually, in 995, they found a safe place on a rocky piece of land almost surrounded by the river Wear. It was here in 998 a building called 'the White Church' was built and dedicated. Twenty years later it was finished except for the western towers.

This magnificently beautiful building, looking down over Durham, not only possesses the body of St Cuthbert and the remains of his coffin made in 698, but also the bones of the saintly scholar, Venerable Bede, and a collection of relics of northern saints. See also page 20.

TATIE CAKE

This would be a typical high tea dish in the workers' houses on the right of the photograph. Originally it had pastry top and bottom, but in these diet-conscious days I have put it only on top.

Shortcrust pastry made from:

100 g (4 oz) flour and 50 g (2 oz) margarine	4 medium size potatoes, half cooked
175 g (6 oz) lean bacon, chopped	a pinch of dried sage
1 medium onion, finely sliced	1 tablespoon milk
salt and pepper	

Serves 4

Put a layer of sliced potatoes at the bottom of a shallow greased dish. Lay the chopped bacon on top and finish with the onion and sage. Season to taste and pour over the milk. Roll out the pastry to fit and press on. Brush over with milk and prick over the top. Bake at 190°C, 375°F, Gas Mark 5 for about 35–45 minutes.

HARVO BREAD

600 ml (1 pint) water	225 g (8 oz) sultanas
450 g (1 lb) sugar	225 g (8 oz) wholemeal flour
225 g (8 oz) margarine	225 g (8 oz) plain white flour
225 g (8 oz) cooking dates	1 rounded teaspoon bicarbonate of soda

Makes 3 small loaves

Put the water, sugar, margarine, dates and sultanas in a saucepan. Bring to boil, stirring, then allow to cool. Add the rest of the ingredients in order given and mix well. Put into three 450 g (1 lb) loaf tins and bake at 180°C, 350°F, Gas Mark 4 for 35 minutes, then lower to 150°C, 300°F, Gas Mark 1 for about 40 minutes. Cool on a rack and wrap in a towel when cool.

Durham Cathedral and Castle surrounded by Durham Town, c. 1920s (by kind permission of The Dean and Chapter of Durham Cathedral).

BEEF CECILS

In 1823 a partnership was formed between Mr John Wheeley Lea, a druggist, and Mr William Perrins, a chemist, who pooled their resources to develop their drug store at 68 Broad Street, Worcester. They sold groceries, cosmetics and toilet articles in addition to pharmaceuticals, and marketed several of their own preparations in that line. In 1835, Lord Sandys, who had recently returned from India, approached them to make up an Indian sauce recipe for him. In addition to Lord Sandys's order they also made a few jars for their own use, but on tasting it, found it so unpalatable it was consigned to the cellar and forgotten.

Some years later they came across these jars but before throwing them out, they tasted the sauce again and found it matured and delicious. Thus Lea and Perrins set about making this original sauce in 1837 from the Indian recipe and so it has remained. The formula and process are still secret except for a very few people concerned with making it. Worcestershire sauce is both original and highly thought of all over the world and considered one of Britain's great culinary inventions. It is exported to all corners of the earth.

The roller-conveyor shown in the photograph was very new in 1896 and it took the export cases in a spiral right down to the waiting wagons and, later, lorries for despatch.

Lea and Perrins Export Department, Worcester, c. 1896.

BEEF CECILS

Cecils are the early 19th-century name for rounds of minced beef flavoured with anchovies, lemon and Worcestershire sauce. They were originally rolled in egg and breadcrumbs and fried, and can still be made that way.

450 g (1 lb) lean, raw minced beef
1 medium onion, finely chopped
50 g (2 oz) white breadcrumbs
grated rind of $\frac{1}{2}$ large lemon
salt and pepper

4 anchovy fillets, drained & chopped
1 tablespoon parsley, chopped
1 tablespoon Worcestershire sauce
1 egg, beaten
25 g (1 oz) butter

Serves 4

Mix all ingredients except the butter in a bowl and fold in well. Divide the mixture into 12 balls, then shape into flat round cakes. At this point you can either roll them in beaten egg and breadcrumbs and deep fry, or heat the butter in a pan and fry several at a time until golden brown on each side, about 7–10 minutes. They can be served either with a wedge of lemon or a few drops of Worcestershire sauce, puréed potatoes and a green vegetable.

LEG OF LAMB OR MUTTON WITH CAPER SAUCE

Royal Sovereign, *first of a new class of battleship, was built at Ports-mouth, work commencing in September 1889 and completed in 1892. She was 380 feet long with triple-expansion compound engines of 13,000 horsepower, giving her a speed of 17½ knots. Her principal armament consisted of four 13½ inch breech-loading 67-ton rifles mounted in armoured barbettes for'ard and aft.*

As can be seen from the photograph, these guns were mounted in the open without armoured turrets. Some of the secondary armament of quick-firing guns is seen on the lower bridge and in the for'ard top. Also the funnels are abreast instead of in line.

The food on such a vessel would have been better than any served on board a ship on active service. Fresh meats and vegetables were freely available. Lamb or mutton was of very good quality and often served like this:

LEG OF LAMB OR MUTTON WITH CAPER SAUCE

2 kg (4½ lb) leg of lamb or
   mutton
4 medium carrots, sliced
2 large onions, sliced
2 leeks, if available, chopped
a sprig of thyme and parsley
salt and pepper

For the sauce
2 tablespoons butter
2 heaped tablespoons flour
850 ml (1½ pints) lamb stock
4 tablespoons capers, drained
2 teaspoons parsley, chopped
3 tablespoons double cream

Serves about 8

Put the meat into a large saucepan and barely cover with cold water. Bring to the boil and skim off any scum. Add the vegetables, the herbs and seasonings. Bring back to the boil, then simmer gently for 30 minutes to the pound, or until tender. Leave in the stock until cold, then remove fat from the top.

To make the sauce, measure out the amount of stock you will need and warm it. Melt the butter, stir in the flour and cook for 1 minute. Then gradually add the warm stock, stirring all the time until smooth and thickened. Add the capers and the parsley and taste for seasonings. Finally stir in the cream, re-heat but do not reboil. Heat up the meat, then lift it out and cut into fairly thick slices and serve a little sauce over it, the rest separately. Serve freshly cooked root vegetables with it.

The stock will make good mutton broth with a few additions.

Royal Sovereign, *off Portsmouth, Hampshire, 1893.*

CHEESE AND ONION PIE

Derby is an ancient town on the river Derwent with a fine cathedral built in Henry VIII's reign, but rebuilt in 1725 by James Gibb. Inside is the tomb of Bess of Hardwick (see page 127). Porcelain was first made here in 1756 by William Duesbury to whom George III gave the right to use the Crown insignia and call it Crown Derby.

Rolls Royce opened its car-manufacturing works here in 1908 for the making of the famous car, and Rolls Royce aero engines are among many exhibits in the Industrial Museum.

Derby also makes one of the rarer English cheeses. The first English cheese factory was established at Longford in 1870, but the industry had been carried on in farm houses for centuries. Derby cheese has a flaky grain and a smooth, milky flavour, more buttery than a Cheddar. Sage Derby is also made, with green blotches running through it caused by the addition of sage.

CHEESE AND ONION PIE

A recipe from a cook who worked at one of the large Derbyshire houses all her life.

Pastry	Filling
225 g (8 oz) self-raising flour	2 large onions, grated
½ teaspoon salt	225 g (8 oz) cheese, Sage Derby
50 g (2 oz) butter	or strong Cheddar
50 g (2 oz) lard	salt, pepper and nutmeg
2–3 tablespoons cold water	300 ml (½ pint) double cream
	a little milk

Serves 4–6

First make the pastry and let it rest. Then roll it out and divide in half to fit a 20 cm (8 in) flat pie dish. Line the bottom and prick lightly. Lay on the grated onions and cheese, then season the cream and mix well. Whip it lightly, then pour it over the top.

Pre-heat the oven to 190°C, 375°F, Gas Mark 5. Lay the other piece of pastry over the top, after damping the edges, and press down, fluting them. Brush with a little milk and bake for about 35–40 minutes.

It is a simple and delicious dish which makes a good lunch or supper: or it can be excellent with cold ham or pork.

Celebrations in Cornmarket, Derby, looking toward Market Place, July 16, 1881, for the opening of the Royal Agricultural Show by the Prince and Princess of Wales.

SHREWSBURY BISCUITS

These little biscuits have been in existence since the 16th century when they were known as Shrewsbury cakes. Famous people who visited the town were offered them and at one time they were also served after funerals. In the 19th century the baker, Palin, made them and they were stamped with a circle saying, 'Palin's Original Shrewsbury Cakes'.

150 g (5 oz) butter, at room temperature
finely grated rind of 1 lemon
100 g (4 oz) castor sugar
2 egg yolks

225 g (8 oz) self-raising flour, sifted
1 rounded tablespoon caraway seeds *or* 50 g (2 oz) currants
sugar for sprinkling

Makes about 28 biscuits

Cream the butter and lemon rind, add sugar and cream thoroughly again. Beat in the egg yolks singly. Then add sifted flour, kneading lightly. Roll into a ball and chill for 1 hour.

Turn out on to a lightly floured surface and roll out, to about ½ cm (¼ in) thick and cut into 6.5 cm (2½ in) circles. Sprinkle with sugar, preferably castor, and put on to a greased or non-stick baking sheet, or one which is covered with Bakewell paper. Pre-heat oven to 180°C, 350°F, Gas Mark 4 and cook for 15–18 minutes or until a pale gold, do not let them darken.

SOUL CAKES

In the 19th century young people went 'a-souling' on All Saints' Day and All Souls' Day at the beginning of November. It took the place of Hallowe'en in Shropshire, Cheshire and Yorkshire, and a soul cake or a little gift of food was expected.

2 teaspoons fresh yeast
450 g (1 lb) flour
100 g (4 oz) butter
225 g (8 oz) sugar

milk to make a soft dough
2 eggs
1 teaspoon mixed spice & a few grains of saffron, soaked

Cream the yeast with a little sugar, rub the fat into the flour and add all dry ingredients and eggs. Pour the yeast into the middle, mix slightly, and add milk and saffron to make dough. Cover and leave in a warm place to rise for about 1 hour. Then turn out, knead again and shape into flat cakes, put on to a lightly greased tray, leave for ½ hour, then bake at 200°C, 400°F, Gas Mark 6 for 15 minutes. Then lower heat to 180°C, 350°F, Gas Mark 4 and continue cooking for a further 15 minutes.

Caryl Bagot (later Lord Bagot) and his sister play cricket with the servants on the lawn at the Rectory, Stanton Lacy, near Ludlow, Shropshire, 1887.
Photograph by courtesy Nancy, Lady Bagot. See also page 100.

NORTHUMBERLAND SINGING HINNIE

George Stephenson was born at Wylam, near Newcastle in 1781, the second son of Robert, fireman of a colliery engine. As a boy he worked as a cowherd, then drove a gin-horse at the colliery. Until his 17th year he was illiterate, but went to night-school where he made rapid progress. In 1812 he was appointed engine-wright at the High Pit, Killingworth at £100 a year. Here he devised his miners' safety lamp, at the same time as Sir Humphry Davy which caused controversy as to which was first. He then designed the 'travelling engine' for the tramroads between the colliery which ran a successful trial in July 1814. In 1822, he impressed the board of the new Stockton and Darlington railway and was able to carry out his own plans using steam instead of animal traction, the result being the opening in September 1825 of the first railway by which public passengers and goods were carried by locomotive. This led to his employment in construction of the Liverpool and Manchester railway. In October 1829 his engine 'The Rocket' (now on show at Bank Top station, Darlington) met with approval.

Subsequently, Stephenson was engineer of, among others, the Grand Junction, the London and Birmingham (with son Robert), Manchester to Leeds, Derby to Birmingham and Normanton to York railways. He was also consulted in Belgium and Spain. He died, in 1848, at Tapton House, Chesterfield, where he had retired.

NORTHUMBERLAND SINGING HINNIE

These are so-called because of the noise they make while cooking. 'Hinnie' is a corruption of honey, a north country term of endearment for children. Formerly made on a griddle, they can also be made in a heavy frying pan.

225 g (8 oz) plain flour	75 g (3 oz) currants
pinch of salt	1 teaspoon baking powder
50 g (2 oz) butter	milk, or better still, sour cream,
50 g (2 oz) lard	to mix
50 g (2 oz) sugar, optional	

Sift the flour, baking powder and salt and rub in fats. Add currants and sugar, then stir well. Mix to a stiff paste with milk or sour cream and roll into a ball.

Heat and lightly grease the griddle or a heavy pan. Squash the round, flat cake about 1 cm ($\frac{1}{2}$ in) thick in the centre of the hot pan. Prick all over with a fork and cook for about 5 minutes on each side. Serve very hot split, with lots of butter. Cut or pull into portions.

Interior of cottage where George Stephenson was born 1781, part of the four-roomed Street House, Wylam, near Newcastle on Tyne, c. 1900. It is a typical single-roomed dwelling in which large families were often brought up in the 18th and 19th centuries.

ALMOND CAKE

The Abbot's Bromley Horn Dance takes place once a year on the Monday after the first Sunday after the fourth of September. The dancers consist of a band of twelve, by tradition, always male. Six men carry the six reindeer antlers on their shoulders, accompanied by Maid Marian, the Hobby Horse, the Fool, a boy carrying a bow and arrow and another a triangle which he beats in time. Also a musician, formerly a fiddler, nowadays an accordion. The men collect the horns (which have been carbon-dated back to about 1065AD), at about 8 a.m. They are then 'danced' around the church (where they are kept), through the village and some farms, until they reach Blithfield Hall (pronounced Bliffield), home of Nancy, Lady Bagot, arriving there about midday. After refreshments they are danced back again and around other farms, returning to the village at teatime, and finally ending back at the church at dusk. It was to commemorate the hunting rights of nearby Needwood Forest.

Nobody quite knows the date of this curious dance, but it is thought by some to date from pre-Christian times. The earliest written reference is 1686, in Plot's Natural History of Staffordshire. The trousers in this photograph were made from the vicarage curtains because they were the traditional colours. However, in 1948 Lord and Lady Bagot provided the present costumes in the Bagot colours of blue and gold. Blithfield Hall has been lived in since its entry into the Domesday Book of 1086, but it became the home of the Bagot family in 1360. Nancy, Lady Bagot, lives there with her daughter.

ALMOND CAKE

Recipe courtesy of Nancy, Lady Bagot, from a handwritten book by Mrs Whieldon, the cook at Blithfield, 1888. Perhaps at one time the dancers were offered a slice of this delicious almond cake? I have halved the quantities to make a medium sized cake.

175 g (6 oz) butter	100 g (4 oz) mixed peel, finely
175 g (6 oz) castor sugar	chopped
4 eggs or 3 large eggs, beaten	25 g (1 oz) ground almonds
175 g (6 oz) flour, sifted	100 g (4 oz) finely chopped
	almonds

Base line a 18 cm (7 in) cake tin and pre-heat oven to 180°C, 350°F, Gas Mark 4. Work the butter until it is a cream, then add the sugar and cream the two together, until light and fluffy. Add the beaten eggs gradually, with a teaspoon of flour after each addition, then fold in the remaining flour. Add chopped peel and almonds and mix very well. Pour into the prepared cake tin and bake in the pre-heated oven for 1½–2 hours, testing before taking out. Cool for a few minutes before lifting out and putting on a wire rack.

The Abbot's Bromley Horn Dancers, Blithfield, Staffordshire, 1880s. Photograph by courtesy of Nancy, Lady Bagot.

BAKEWELL PUDDING

Monsal Dale is about four miles from Bakewell on the River Wye. Fir Cop is behind, with an ancient old British fortress on the top of the hill. It is an extremely beautiful part of England. Also in Derbyshire, is Buxton, standing nearly 1,000 feet above sea level and a centre for exploring the Peak District. It has a hot spring gushing from the belly of the earth. It is also notable for the baths which were built here for the Roman garrison, where the town of Letocetum once stood, with a complicated system of flues for heating the floors, still clearly visible.

At Tissington, in Derbyshire, the wells are 'dressed' on Ascension Day. This is thought to perpetuate a pagan ceremony to propitiate the gods of water. See Chatsworth, page 127.

BAKEWELL PUDDING

Although this is what we would call a tart, it must never be called that at Bakewell. Traditionally it should be baked in an oval dish with sloping sides, but it is more often done in a round one. It is still very popular and is sold at Bloomers in Matlock Street, Bakewell, and also at the Original Bakewell Pudding Shop in the Square.

225 g (8 oz) pastry, either puff or rich shortcrust	100 g (4 oz) butter
	1008 g (4 oz) sugar
2–3 tablespoons raspberry, strawberry or cherry jam	4 eggs
	100 g (4 oz) ground almonds

Serves 4–6

Butter an oval or round dish about 20 cm (8 in) across. Pre-heat the oven to 200°C, 400°F, Gas Mark 6. Roll out the pastry and line the dish with it, keeping back a little for lattice strips, then spread the jam evenly over the base. Melt the butter, leave to cool slightly. Beat eggs with the sugar until a thick cream. Slowly pour butter in, stirring well. Then fold in the almonds. Spread this mixture over the jam evenly. Roll out the pastry trimmings and cut into strips to make a lattice over the top. Dampen the edges so they stick.

Put into the pre-heated oven for 30 minutes until set and gently brown. Serve warm or cold.

A charming model at Monsal Dale, Peak District, Derbyshire, 1870s.

SUSSEX STEWED STEAK

One of the oldest, if not the oldest inn in Sussex, the Star at Alfriston dates from the early 15th century. It was probably a pilgrim's inn, offering shelter to pilgrims on their way to the shrine of St Richard at Chichester. The roof is of half-hundredweight slabs of colourful Horsham stone; the lion at the corner was the figurehead of a ship wrecked off the neighbouring coast over 300 years ago. Underneath the oriel windows are other carvings of snakes and a shield, and the mitred figure of an abbot or bishop, probably St Giles. This inn was built to be an inn about the time of the Battle of Agincourt and has continued so for 500 years.

The village has smuggling traditions and there is also a 14th-century priest's house, with a fine roof.

SUSSEX STEWED STEAK

1.1 kg (2½ lb) good braising steak like chuck or rump, sliced
seasoned flour
salt and black pepper
1 large onion, sliced
150 ml (¼ pint) stout
150 ml (¼ pint) port
150 ml (¼ pint) good beef stock
2 tablespoons mushroom ketchup or walnut ketchup (both made by Keddie Ltd for George Watkins)

Serves 6

Rub the steak with the seasoned flour and add a little more pepper. Lay the pieces so that they are flat in one layer in an ovenproof dish. Slice the onion on top of it in another layer. Then pour in the stout, wine, ketchup and stock.

Cover the dish tightly, with a lid or with foil, and put it into a 150°C, 300°F, Gas Mark 2 oven for 2½–3 hours. Do not hurry it as the long, slow cooking gives a marvellous flavour. Serve with lightly cooked field mushrooms and well-mashed potatoes.

The Star Inn, Alfriston, East Sussex, c. 1870s.

BURLEY HALL QUEEN CAKES

Rutland, once one of the smallest and most attractive of English counties, has now been absorbed into Leicestershire. There are many beautiful buildings, especially early churches such as the Elizabethan church at Brooke which is full of Elizabethan woodwork. At Great Casterton there is a 13th-century church with a square Norman font, also Roman remains as well as Saxon treasure in Market Overton. Uppingham, the public school founded at the end of the 16th century, is in the town of the same name.

Burley-on-the-Hill has a grand mansion once owned by George, Duke of Buckingham, where Ben Jonson, the Elizabethan dramatist, staged a masque. Although twice destroyed, it has been twice rebuilt and has a beautiful front of columns and Doric capitals.

BURLEY HALL QUEEN CAKES

225 g (8 oz) butter, soft
225 g (8 oz) castor sugar
350 g (12 oz) self-raising flour
4 eggs

grated rind 1 lemon
2 teaspoons rosewater
  (obtainable from chemists)

Makes about 12–15 cakes

Pre-heat the oven to 200°C, 400°F, Gas Mark 6. Cream the butter and sugar until light coloured and creamy. Add each egg with the addition of a spoonful of flour, mixing gently. Then add remainder of flour and mix well.

Add the lemon rind, grated finely, with the rosewater, and mix again. Lightly grease a bun tin and spoon the mixture into it. Bake on the top shelf of the pre-heated oven for about 10 minutes.

Take from the tin when cooked and cool on a wire tray.

Tea party at the Rectory, Narbinsthorp, Rutland (now Leicestershire), c. 1900.

CLOTTED CREAM

The excellence of Cornish cream has been known for centuries. It is usually 'clotted' with a rich taste and is very thick, served with buns (called 'splits') and jam, junkets and tarts. It is also put into many savoury dishes, like pork and leek pies.

'They scald their cream and milk in most parts of these counties, and so it is a sort of clouted cream as we we call it, with a little sugar, and so put it on top of the apple pie.'
  (*Through England on a Side-Saddle, Celia Fiennes, 1662–1741*)

CLOTTED CREAM

Set very fresh milk to stand in a wide earthenware pan with handles, for twelve hours in summer, or twenty-four hours in winter. Then lift on to the stove and heat slowly, never allowing it to boil, until the shape of the bottom of the pan is outlined in the cream as a circle concentric to the rim. Without shaking the pan, remove from the heat and leave to cool for twelve hours in a cool place.

The thick crust of cream is then skimmed off with a large spoon or slice. The top will be a golden yellow and very creamy underneath.

CORNISH SPLITS

300 ml (½ pint) milk, tepid	450 g (1 lb) flour
1 teaspoon castor sugar	pinch of salt
25 g (1 oz) fresh yeast, or	50 g (2 oz) lard or butter
12 g (½ oz) dried	

Makes about 12

Warm the milk to blood heat, 36.6°C, 98.4°F. Cream the sugar and yeast together until it froths, and add the milk. Sieve the flour and salt, rub in the fat until like fine breadcrumbs and make a well in the middle. Pour the yeast mixture into this and cover with a cloth. Then knead thoroughly to form a soft dough. Leave covered in a warm place for about 1 hour to double in size and knead again.

Pre-heat oven to 200°C, 400°F, Gas Mark 6 and lightly flour a baking sheet. Shape the dough into small buns and lay on the baking sheet, spaced apart. Leave again for about 20–30 minutes to prove once more, then bake in the pre-heated oven for about 15 minutes. They will sound hollow when tapped on the bottom if cooked.

They can be served hot, cut open and buttered, or cold, split and spread with clotted cream and raspberry or strawberry jam.

Milking the cows, Trewhella, Cornwall, 1900.

MANCHESTER PUDDING

The women in the photograph are engaged in finishing many different kinds of hats, some tropical. Their working conditions do not look too bad, with large windows letting in light and air during the summer. Luton in Bedfordshire was the renowned place for making straw hats.

MANCHESTER PUDDING

This would be a delicious pudding for the summer or winter months. Sometimes it was put into a puff pastry flan case, but it is very good as a light pudding without. If making with the puff pastry case, the jam is spread on top of it first.

25 g (1 oz) butter
600 ml (1 pint) milk
50 g (2 oz) castor sugar
grated rind of 1 lemon
75 g (3 oz) fresh white
 breadcrumbs

2 large eggs, separated
3 tablespoons brandy or sweet
 sherry
4–5 tablespoons apricot,
 strawberry or other jam
a little butter for greasing

Serves 4–6

Melt the butter in a saucepan, add the milk and sugar. Let it dissolve by stirring well. Then add the breadcrumbs and lemon rind and bring to the boil then simmer for 3–4 minutes. Take from the heat. Beat the egg yolks and add a little of the boiled milk mixture to them, then tip into the mixture and stir continuously over a very gentle heat until it thickens slightly. On no account let it boil, it should run off the back of the wooden spoon in ribbons.

Warm the brandy or sherry to a low heat with the jam. Lightly grease a flameproof serving dish, about 1 litre (2 pint) capacity, and pour the jam on the bottom, then add the egg yolk mixture and put into a 180°C, 350°F, Gas Mark 4 oven for about 20 minutes.

Meanwhile, whisk the egg whites until stiff adding a little sugar if liked. Take pudding out of the oven and spread the egg mixture evenly over the top. Lower the heat to 170°C, 325°F, Gas Mark 3 and continue cooking for 15–20 minutes until risen and slightly golden.

This pudding can be eaten hot or cold.

Women doing the finishing process in a man's hat factory, Manchester, July 1909.

OXFORD SAUSAGES

OXFORD SAUSAGES

These sausages are delicate and delicious as they are made with pork and veal. They are particularly suitable for making at home, as they are skinless. This is an 18th-century recipe and makes about 16 sausages.

225 g (8 oz) lean pork	grated rind of $\frac{1}{2}$ large lemon
225 g (8 oz) pie veal	$\frac{1}{2}$ teaspoon dried sage
150 g (5 oz) brown breadcrumbs	$\frac{1}{2}$ teaspoon dried thyme
200 g (7 oz) shredded suet	$\frac{1}{2}$ teaspoon grated nutmeg
1 level teaspoon salt	freshly ground black pepper

Trim the meats so that no gristly pieces are left. Then mince them both finely. Put them through twice if you like a finer texture. Add the breadcrumbs and moisten with 2 tablespoons water. Mix well, then add the lemon rind, suet, nutmeg, herbs, salt and pepper, using about $\frac{1}{4}$ teaspoon of the latter. Mix again.

Flour your hands and form the mixture into sausage shapes to the size you like. Then place them on a lightly floured dish or board. They can be chilled until you need to cook them.

Heat up either a little oil or butter, or a mixture, and when it is hot but not too hot, fry each sausage for about 5 minutes on each side or until it is golden brown and a little crusty.

They are delicious served either for breakfast with eggs and bacon, or for a luncheon with butter beans and onions.

First eight of Magdalen College, in front of Magdalen College barge, Oxford, 1919. (Photographer, R. C. Gregg)

RICHMOND MAIDS OF HONOUR

RICHMOND MAIDS OF HONOUR

These little almond cakes are said to have been first made at Richmond Palace when Henry VIII was king. The young girl who first made them gave her recipe to a Mr Billet, who, after her death, opened a 'Maids of Honour' shop in Richmond. The secret was kept in the family for many generations. However, a great-great-grandson of his, a Mr Newen, went to work in Mr Billet's shop and bought the recipe from the owner for a thousand guineas. Later he opened his own shop in Richmond to make them.

The present Mr Newen still makes them by hand at 288 Kew Road, Kew Gardens.

450 g (1 lb) prepared puff pastry	2 tablespoons brandy
225 g (8 oz) curd or ricotta cheese	2 tablespoons breadcrumbs, level
175 g (6 oz) warmed butter	50 g (2 oz) ground almonds
2 egg yolks	1 lemon
100 g (4 oz) castor sugar	freshly grated nutmeg

This amount makes about 24 cakes

Roll out the pastry on a lightly floured surface and use to line 24 bun tins. Light the oven at 200°C, 400°F, Gas Mark 6.

Break up the curds with a fork and work in the softened butter. Beat the egg yolks, sugar and brandy in a small bowl and beat in the breadcrumbs, then add the ground almonds to this. Grate the lemon, squeeze out the juice and add this to the mixture with the nutmeg.

Mix well and spoon into the pastry cases, half filling each one as the mixture rises. Bake in the centre of the pre-heated oven for 15 minutes, then lower the heat to 180°C, 350°F, Gas Mark 4 for a further 15 minutes or until set and pale gold in colour.

Punts on the Thames at Richmond, 1869.

NOTTINGHAM PUDDING

Goose Fair takes place on the first Thursday in October: the photographer records that October 1908 experienced a heat weave. The fair originated in the 13th century, so-called because of the large numbers of geese sold there before Michaelmas. Before the calendar changed it was on October 10, but nowadays Goose Fair is still held on the first Thursday in October and goes on for three days. There are several traditional foods eaten at that time, such as 'mushy' peas (a purée of dried peas) with mint sauce, brandysnaps (see page 36), Grantham gingerbreads (see page 119), Mansfield pie (a pork pie glazed with redcurrant jelly) and Nottingham pudding.

Whoso eats goose on Michaelmas Day
Shall never lack money his debts to pay.

NOTTINGHAM PUDDING

A traditional recipe adapted from the 19th century. The Bramley cooking apple originated in Southwell, Nottinghamshire and the original tree still flourishes in a garden at Bramley Tree Cottage, in this town, with its great Norman minster. Lord Byron used to spend his holidays at Burgage Manor, Southwell.

6 medium, even-sized Bramley apples	6 tablespoons flour
75 g (3 oz) butter	3 eggs
75 g (3 oz) castor sugar	approx. 300 ml (½ pint) milk
a pinch each of nutmeg and cloves	pinch of salt

Serves 6

Peel and core apples and keep in salted water until needed. Cream butter and sugar until light and add nutmeg and cloves. Fill the centre of the drained apples with this mixture. Put in a well-buttered ovenproof dish. Blend flour with a little cold water, add the well-beaten eggs and a pinch of salt. Then add enough milk to make a thick, creamy batter. Pour over the apples and bake in a pre-heated oven at 180°C, 350°F, Gas Mark 4 for 1½ hours. Serve with whipped cream.

MANSFIELD PUDDING

Mansfield was once a small settlement in Sherwood Forest. This pudding was sold at Mansfield Fair annually. A Gooseberry Pie is also made with hot water crust, see page 79.

50 g (2 oz) fresh white breadcrumbs	25 g (1 oz) sugar, or to taste
75 g (3 oz) plain flour	75 g (3 oz) currants
75 g (3 oz) shredded suet or melted butter	2 eggs, large
	300 ml (½ pint) milk
1 level teaspoon nutmeg	1 tablespoon brandy or sherry

Serves 4–6

Mix all dry ingredients (or melted butter), beat the eggs with the milk and brandy then pour into the dry ingredients, mixing well. Butter an ovenproof pie dish, pour the mixture in and bake for 1 hour at 180°C, 350°F, Gas Mark 4. Serve with cream.

Goose Fair, Nottingham, October 1908, looking east from Beastmarket Hill.

THE SANDRINGHAM

GILBERT & SON LTD

GRANTHAM GINGERBREADS

The New York referred to, is in the Lincolnshire fens, the journey being arranged to transport the mail to certain fen villages between Lincoln and Boston and the health resort Woodhall Spa, there being no train service on that day. It was the time of the Boer War and Queen Victoria had expressed a wish that all Christmas letters from relatives fighting should be delivered in time. The postmaster, Mr J. T. Walker, approached Mr Gilbert, owner of a motor engineers in Lincoln, and although the car was at King's Lynn, he brought it up with only two days' notice and at once undertook to make the journey. The car was a Daimler 'Rougemont' Waggonette, $5\frac{1}{2}$ BHP which was driven by Mr Gilbert, the mails being in charge of a Post Office official, Mr Alex Taylor. They carried a half a ton of mail and left Lincoln at 7.40 a.m. amidst well wishers.

The roads were very bad and, at one point, at Five Mile House Ferry, the car and mails were ferried over the River Witham to the Fiskerton side. Some mail for villages not on the route was transferred to local postmen who had a pony and trap. The car reached New York at 11.20 a.m. having completed thirty-four miles over some of the worst roads in Lincolnshire, in three hours and forty minutes. The New York postmaster, Mr S. Joll, invited them to share his Christmas dinner. The return journey was arranged so as to pick up mails on the way back. A long stop was made waiting for mail from North and South Kyme. Atchinson gave them tea as the night was bitterly cold and they reached Lincoln again at 6.45 p.m. for the night mails. This experimental service was a decided success and Mr Gilbert was congratulated heartily for what is believed to have been the first Motor Service arranged for conveying Her Majesty's Mails in the provinces.

GRANTHAM GINGERBREADS

Let us hope that the travellers were given some of these delicious biscuits with their tea! They are not in the least like most gingerbreads, being pale and hollow, a little like a meringue. They were first made by a William Egglestone, a baker, in 1740, who made a mistake in the cake ingredients and produced these instead, which have been popular ever since. They are now sold by Catlin's Café, High Street, Grantham.

225 g (8 oz) self-raising flour, sifted
1 teaspoon ground ginger
100 g (4 oz) butter, at room temperature

225 g (8 oz) castor sugar
1 large egg

Sieve the flour and ginger. Mash butter and thoroughly mix in the sugar and beaten egg. Add flour mixture. Work by hand to a dry, stiff dough, do not add any liquid except egg. Roll into small balls and put on to non-stick baking tray or Bakewell paper, leaving room between them. Press down and bake at 150°C, 300°F, Gas Mark 2 for 30–45 minutes. Do not colour them. Leave to cool and harden before taking off tray, as they are apt to crack if warm.

The first delivery in England of mail by motor car, Christmas Day, 1899, Lincoln to New York, Lincolnshire.

WHOLEMEAL APPLE SCONES

Ploughing by oxen was not all that unusual in parts of England, for it went on until well into the 20th century. However, a team of four such fine-looking beasts was not general; more often there would be a team of two. This experiment was also tried during World War II in England, when petrol was scarce.

WHOLEMEAL APPLE SCONES

225 g (8 oz) wholemeal flour
4 level tablespoons baking
   powder
pinch of salt
50 g (2 oz) warm butter

2 rounded tablespoons grated
   apple
approx. 150 ml (¼ pint) milk
1 egg

Makes about 10

Pre-heat oven to 200°C, 400°F, Gas Mark 6 and lightly grease a baking tray. Combine the flour, baking powder and salt. Rub in the butter and stir in the grated apple. Beat the milk and egg together and gradually add enough of this to the flour to make a pliable, soft dough. Turn on to a floured surface and knead slightly.

Now, you can either roll it out and cut into 5 cm (2 in) rounds, or shape into one large flat cake, marking it into 8 or 10 wedges. Put on to the greased baking sheet, brush tops over with the remaining egg and milk and bake in the centre of the oven for about 15–20 minutes.

A pinch of ground cloves can be added if liked.

OAT BISCUITS

These are delicious with butter and cheese.

225 g (8 oz) plain flour
225 g (8 oz) porridge oats
50 g (2 oz) castor sugar
75 g (3 oz) butter or margarine

75 g (3 oz) lard
½ teaspoon salt
½ teaspoon bicarbonate of soda

Makes about 12–15

Sift flour with salt and bicarbonate of soda. Rub fats into this, add the oats and sugar, and mix gradually with a little milk until a firm dough. Roll out thinly on a floured surface, and cut into 6 cm (2½ in) rounds. Bake at 200°C, 400°F, Gas Mark 6 on a greased baking sheet for about 10 minutes. Take off when cooked and, when cool, store in an airtight tin.

Ploughing with oxen in Sussex, 1870s.

LAMB'S WOOL

Shepton Mallet is a market town and the permanent site of the Royal Bath and West Agricultural Show. Cider and brewing are some of its chief industries, as well as the sale of agricultural machinery. Most of its wealth originally came from the wool trade which made it famous for cloth and stockings. The museum there houses many discoveries from the nearby Mendip Caves. Note the beautiful hexagonal market cross, c. 1500.

'On St James's Day the apples are christened', is an old Somerset saying.

The apples in some Somerset towns are 'wassailed' on the old calendar Twelfth Night, January 17, to ward off evil spirits from harming the apple crops. The word comes from the Anglo-Saxon was hail, meaning 'good health'. Pieces of toast were floated in the wassail bowl, hence the term 'toasting'. The apple harvest goes on until November and when the apples are picked, the tiny ones are left on for the pixies. On Christmas Eve a drink is served called Lamb's Wool.

LAMB'S WOOL

Serves about 8

Stick about 8 cloves into 8 medium sized apples, then put into a bowl and bake them with a very little water in a hot oven, 200°C, 400°F, Gas Mark 6 until they are soft, but not mushy. Put them in the bowl you will serve the drink from. Meanwhile heat up 4.5 litres (1 gallon) strong dark beer with a 2.5 cm (1 in) piece of cinnamon, 6 allspice berries and about 1 rounded tablespoon sugar. Do not boil it or the alcohol will evaporate. Pour this, hot, through a strainer over the apples and serve. Nuts, hot apple cakes and spiced cakes are eaten with this drink.

SOMERSET APPLE CAKE

100 g (4 oz) butter	pinch ground ginger
225 g (8 oz) self-raising flour	2 eggs, beaten
100 g (4 oz) brown sugar	a little cider or milk
2 medium-sized cooking apples, peeled & chopped	castor sugar for sprinkling

Rub the butter into the flour then add the sugar. Add the finely chopped apples and the ginger. Make a well in the middle, pour in the well-beaten eggs to mix it to a paste. Then add slowly, just enough cider or milk to make a firm but not too wet mixture that leaves the sides of the bowl clean. Pre-heat the oven to 190°C, 375°F, Gas Mark 5 and lightly butter and flour a tin. Put the mixture into it, smoothing over the surface and bake for about 1 hour, but test before taking out.

Sprinkle with castor sugar and serve warm with cream, or cold.

The Reverend Saunders with his camera, Market Place, Shepton Mallet, Somerset, c. 1890s.

ROAST AND STUFFED AYLESBURY DUCK

Aylesbury ducks have always been considered the finest for cooking. They are unequalled in taste and much heavier than many others. Indeed, it is said that the rapid growth of the ducklings can often exceed over 2 kg (4½lb) when only about 8 weeks old. The flesh is tender yet full of flavour. Alas, the ducks are no longer bred in Aylesbury except by private owners, but they are bred elsewhere. They are white in colour, look magnificent, but are poor layers.

'The Aylesbury Ducks, are deservedly, a universal favourite. Its snowy plumage and comfortable comportment made it a credit to the poultry yard . . . in parts of Buckinghamshire, this member of the duck family is bred on an extensive scale . . . in the abodes of the cottagers.'
(The Book of Household Management, *Mrs Beeton, 1861.*)

ROAST AND STUFFED AYLESBURY DUCK

These ducks are usually given a fairly tart stuffing and served with either apple sauce or apple rings.

1 Aylesbury duck about 2 kg (4½ lb)
1 lemon
salt and freshly ground pepper
25 g (1 oz) butter
3 medium-sized eating apples
1 bunch watercress
300 ml (½ pint) giblet stock or red wine

For the stuffing
50 g (2 oz) fresh breadcrumbs
2 stalks celery, finely chopped
1 small onion, grated
pinch of dried sage
grated rind of ½ lemon and ½ orange
1 tablespoon each: lemon & orange juice
salt & pepper

Serves 3–4

Wipe the duck, inside and out, then sprinkle with lemon juice inside and out. Make up the stuffing by mixing all the ingredients well and putting it into the body of the bird. Secure with a skewer. Pre-heat the oven to 200°C, 400°F, Gas Mark 6.

Stand the duck on a low trivet if possible, and season. Put into the centre of the oven covered with a piece of foil or greaseproof paper.

After 30 minutes, lower heat to 180°C, 350°F, Gas Mark 4 and pour off any excess fat. Pour off any excess fat every 20 minutes, leaving only pan juices and cook for about 20 minutes to the pound. Baste from time to time.

About 15 minutes before it is cooked, core the apples but do not peel them. Cut into fairly thick slices. Heat up some butter and fry them lightly in it on both sides. Sprinkle a little lemon over and keep warm.

When cooked, lift the duck out on to a warmed dish and keep warm. Add the stock or wine to the de-fatted pan juices and boil up to reduce. Serve the apple rings and watercress separately around the duck and gravy.

High Street, Aylesbury, Buckinghamshire, c. 1891.

PHEASANT WITH WHITE GRAPES

Chatsworth House is, with Haddon Hall and Hardwick Hall (built by Bess of Hardwick), one of the three great Derbyshire mansions. Chatsworth is set in the Peak District and has notable gardens designed by Capability Brown in 1760. The original Elizabethan Hunting Tower and Queen Mary's Bower in the grounds still survive, but the old house was replaced by the present one between 1687 and 1705 by the first Duke of Devonshire. The original estate was acquired by William Cavendish who married the indefatigable builder, Bess of Hardwick, who later became Countess of Shrewsbury and the present baroque mansion was begun by her great-great-grandson. A magnificent sea-horse fountain was designed for the sixth Duke by Joseph Paxton.

'Chatsworth is indeed a most glorious and magnificent house ... it is indeed a palace for a prince. The front to the garden is the most regular piece of architecture I have seen in all the north part of England; the pilaster 72 foot high to the foot of the baluster on the top; the frieze under the cornish (sic) is spacious and has the motto of the family upon it.' A Tour Through the Whole Island of Great Britain, Daniel Defoe, *1724–6.*

PHEASANT WITH WHITE GRAPES

2 well-hung hen pheasants
150 g (5 oz) butter, at room temperature
450 g (1 lb) white grapes, seeded & skinned

2 tablespoons brandy
salt and freshly ground pepper
75 g (3 oz) fresh white breadcrumbs

Serves 6

See the birds are cleaned well, then put them in a roasting tin with 75 g (3 oz) of the butter spread over the breasts and legs. Pre-heat oven to 190°C, 375°F, Gas Mark 5. Cover the birds with greased paper or foil and roast for 20 minutes to the pound and 20 minutes over, basting from time to time.

Meanwhile, peel and seed the grapes and squeeze the juice from half of them. When cooked, take the birds from the oven, lift out and keep hot. Put the grape juice in the pan with the juices and seasoning, scraping down the sides and mixing well. Add the warmed brandy and set it alight, then immediately add the whole grapes. Simmer for 2 minutes. Melt the remaining butter in a frying pan and toss the breadcrumbs in it and brown them very slightly. Sprinkle over the pheasants and serve the grapes and sauce separately. If preferred, the birds can be carved before bringing them to table. In this case, pour a little sauce over them but keep the rest in a sauce boat.

Chatsworth House, Derbyshire, west front, with Duke of Devonshire and child on the lawn, late 1860s. (Photographer J. Warwick.)

CHERRY BUMPERS

Kent, Sir – everbody knows Kent – apples, cherries, hops and women'

(Jingle, in Charles Dickens' The Pickwick Papers)

Daniel Defoe, in his book A Tour through the Whole Island of Great Britain *(1724–26), has this to say about the cherry crop near Maidstone, Kent.*

'*Round this town are the largest cherry orchards, and the most of them that are in any part of England, and the gross of the quantity of cherries, and the best of them which supply the whole city of London come from hence, and are therefore called Kentish cherries.*

CHERRY BUMPERS

These small cherry turnovers are served in early August on Cherry Pie Sunday, which celebrates the end of the cherry picking. They are served hot, straight from the oven, on the baking trays. Sometimes the cherry pickers who only had rather primitive cooking arrangements would make the bumpers between two thick saucers. They were eaten with pints of ale.

For the pastry
225 g (8 oz) plain flour, sifted
pinch of salt
100 g (4 oz) lard or margarine
about 2 tablespoons cold water

Filling
450 g (1 lb) dark, ripe cherries, without stones
75 g (3 oz) castor sugar, or to taste
sugar for sprinkling

Makes about 12

Make the pastry by putting the sifted flour and salt into the mixing bowl, rubbing in the fat until the mixture is like fine breadcrumbs, then adding the cold water, mixing well, to make a stiff dough. Roll into a ball and chill for not less than 30 minutes.

Meanwhile, put the cherries in a bowl and sprinkle with the sugar and leave while the pastry is resting. Then turn out pastry on to a lightly floured surface, roll out and cut into circles 10 cm (4 in) across. Heap some cherries and sugar in the middle of each. Dampen the edges and pinch together on top firmly. Bake in a pre-heated oven at 200°C, 400°F, Gas Mark 6 for 20 minutes, take out and scatter with a little sugar and put back for about 5 minutes to set the sugar. Serve hot, or warm.

OAST CAKES

There are a number of hop-drying kilns all over Kent, for it is a hop-growing centre. The oast house is a pointed, circular building.

225 g (8 oz) self-raising flour
pinch of salt
50 g (2 oz) butter, margarine or lard

75 g (3 oz) currants
1 teaspoon lemon juice and a teaspoon grated rind
deep oil for frying

Makes about 4 cakes

Sift flour into a bowl and add salt. Rub in fat until texture resembles breadcrumbs. Add currants, lemon juice and rind, then mix to a fairly firm dough with about 4 tablespoons water or milk and water. Divide the dough into 4 pieces and put on to a floured surface. Roll into circles and fry in the oil until brown all over. Drain well and eat hot, sprinkled with sugar, brown or white.

'Fair Maids of Kent'

REFORM CLUB CHOPS

Piccadilly Circus presents a different picture in these days. Regent Street is the street ahead with the Café Royal, which had been opened by Daniel Thevenon and his wife Celestine in 1865. Later he changed his name to Nichols which is why the plates and cutlery were stamped with N, not because of Napoleon as many think. To the left and down Piccadilly is St James's Street, known for many famous London clubs, the elegant resorts of most gentlemen. These clubs had extremely fine chefs: the Reform Club acquired the services of the great chef Alexis Soyer in 1837, who was also the author of many books, an inventor and a humanitarian. Soyer wanted, he wrote: 'not to replace the dishes so much in vogue at the Albion (supper rooms in Drury Lane), Simpsons-in-the-Strand, Evans' Cider Cellars and such like places, but to add to their variety without much interfering with the nightly business of such establishments'.

At that time, a late snack could consist of a huge rumpsteak or thick mutton chops grilled over charcoal at a tavern or chop house, the latter often eaten with pickled walnuts, so Soyer invented the Reform Club's own spicy sauce for mutton chops.

REFORM CLUB CHOPS

4 thick loin of lamb chops
freshly ground black pepper
a little softened butter

Sauce

2 tablespoons each: wine
  vinegar & castor sugar
1 tablespoon black peppercorns
1 small onion, finely chopped
300 ml (½ pint) good gravy or
  consommé

2 thin slices chopped ham or
  tongue
2 tablespoons finely sliced
  beetroot
2 gherkins, sliced thin
1 hard-boiled egg white, sliced
  thin

Serves 2 or 4 depending on size

Make the sauce before grilling the chops. Put the vinegar, sugar, crushed peppercorns and finely chopped onion in a pan and cook over a high flame until the onion is soft. Add the gravy or stock and simmer for 5 minutes. Strain, then add all other ingredients. Trim fat from chops and spread both sides with soft butter and pepper, then grill, first under a hot flame, then lower a little to cook as desired. Sprinkle with salt before serving, and serve the sauce, hot, in a sauce boat.

ANGELS ON HORSEBACK

A savoury of oysters rolled in rashers of streaky bacon, grilled or baked until bacon is crisp, then served on hot toast. Allow at least 4 per person.

Piccadilly Circus, London, C. 1880. (Photographer George Washington Wilson.)

MALVERN PUDDING

Great Malvern is situated on the slopes of the Malvern Hills, an impressive range which extends for 9 miles along the Herefordshire border. Water from the Malvern Hills used to be the purest in Britain, due to the hard, pre-Cambrian rocks there. No particles contaminated the water which flows from many springs. This was first discovered by Dr John Wall in 1757. Schweppes have been bottling Malvern Water for over fifty years and several wells, such as Holy Well and St Ann's Well can be seen today. The water from St Ann's Well is now free to all who walk up to it.

At one time the water was thought to have curative powers and a water cure known as hydrotherapy was brought to Malvern by two doctors. At the beginning of the 19th century Malvern became a summer retreat for rich and famous people, such as Jenny Lind, the singer, and Lord Byron.

'I spent the summer vacation of this year among the Malvern Hills. Those were days of romance,' said Lord Byron, 1808.

As the spa became known, a good library, shops, Assembly Rooms and hotels were built. Beauchamp Hotel is still there, looking very much the same, still serving good food.

Fountain of health! in annals of old time,
Named holy. Forever, I could stray
Beside that stream, thou purest spring that flows! (Bloomfield.)

MALVERN PUDDING

From a recipe of 1877.

1 heaped tablespoon cornflour creamed with 2 tablespoons milk
100 g (4 oz) sugar
300 ml (½ pint) milk
3 eggs, beaten

3 tablespoons double cream
450 g (1 lb) apples, chopped
grated rind & juice 1 lemon
150 g (5 oz) sugar, or to taste
a little butter

Serves about 4–6

First cook the peeled, cored and chopped apples with the grated lemon rind and juice, sugar, and about 2–3 tablespoons water. Cook for about 15 minutes or until they are a purée and rather dry. Cool and reserve.

Mix the cornflour with a little cold water, then boil together the sugar and rest of the milk. When boiling, stir it into the basin with the cornflour mixture and go on stirring until it is quite smooth. Cool a little, then mix the cream with the beaten eggs well and stir in. Light the oven to 200°C, 400°F, Gas Mark 6.

Lightly butter an ovenproof dish and pour in half the egg mixture, then lay the apple purée on top and cover with the remaining mixture. Bake in the pre-heated oven for 20–25 minutes. Serve either just warm, or better still, cold.

Outside Beauchamp Hotel, Great Malvern, Worcestershire–Herefordshire border, 1860s.

GOD's KITCHELS

Ipswich is an old city with some old buildings like the Ancient House, Buttermarket, which was built in 1567. Note also the fine carved pillar in the photograph. It was also the birthplace of Cardinal Wolsey but Wolsey's Gate is the only relic of the Cardinal's project to build a college in his birthplace. The old inn, called the Great White Horse, features in Charles Dickens' The Pickwick Papers. *It is where Mr Pickwick made a mistake about the number of his room.*

Suffolk once supplied London with butter from its indigenous Suffolk Dun cow. John Kirby in The Suffolk Traveller *wrote of it: '. . . it is justly esteemed the pleasantest and best in England.'*

There is a Suffolk custom to make pastries, called 'God's Kitchels' between December 25 and January 6 for visiting godchildren. They are not unlike Coventry God-cakes but are more spicy.

'Ask me a blessing and I will give you a kitchel!'

GOD'S KITCHELS

450 g (1 lb) prepared puff pastry	50 g (2 oz) ground almonds
50 g (2 oz) butter	½ teaspoon ground cinnamon
225 g (8 oz) currants	½ teaspoon ground nutmeg
75 g (3 oz) candied peel, chopped	castor sugar to sprinkle

Makes about 12

Roll out the pastry to about 30 cm (12 in) long and 15 cm (6 in) wide, then cut in half evenly. Melt the butter, add the currants, peel, ground almonds, spices and mix very well.

Cover one half of the pastry with this mixture and dampen the edges, then put on the other half of pastry and press down. With the back of a knife mark the top into divisions about 5 cm (2 in) square but do not cut through.

Pre-heat the oven to 220°C, 425°F, Gas Mark 7 and when hot put the cake in and cook for 25–30 minutes or until risen and golden. While still warm sprinkle over with castor sugar and put back in the oven for a few minutes for the sugar to melt. Cut into little cakes before they get cold.

Messenger boys on the corner of Silent Street, Ipswich, Suffolk, c. 1890s.

OXFORD MARMALADE

The front of Christchurch College is on St Aldate's Street and the great gateway is surmounted by a tower begun by Cardinal Wolsey, but only completed in 1682 from designs of Sir Christopher Wren. It contains the huge bell 'Tom' dedicated to St Thomas of Canterbury, which was recast in 1680. It is the largest college in Oxford and has for its chapel the ancient cathedral.

It is referred to as Christchurch, not Christchurch College, and in the university it has become known as 'The House'.

OXFORD MARMALADE

This is a chunky marmalade full of flavour. This quantity makes 5–6 × 450 g (1 lb) jars.

1.4 kg (3 lb) Seville oranges, not too ripe, washed
2 large, juicy lemons
2 litres (3½ pints) water
2.7 kg (6 lb) half white and half brown sugar

or use all white plus 2 × 15 ml spoons (2 tablespoons) black treacle

Wash the oranges well and pick off any stalks, then put them into a large saucepan or preserving pan with 1.7 litres (3 pints) water.

Cover and bring to the boil, then simmer gently for about 1 hour until the peel is soft enough to squeeze between the fingers. At this point they can be left and the marmalade finished later on.

Take a large flat meat dish and take out about 6 oranges at a time with a slotted spoon and cut them in half. With a small spoon scoop out the pips and pith and put this into a smaller saucepan with the remaining 300 ml (½ pint) water. When you have done this, pile the half shells into groups of about 4. Squeeze out the lemon juice, add to the small saucepan, also the half lemon shells. Boil this up, then simmer for about 15 minutes. When ready, strain this liquid into the large saucepan.

Meanwhile, take a sharp knife or half-moon chopper (a luna) and cut down the groups of shells to the size of peel you like. Then tip these into the big pan.

Now comes the important part: add the sugar and it must be stirred over a moderate heat until quite dissolved before boiling up for a set. Any crystals left will cause crystallization when the marmalade is stored. Once dissolved, boil rapidly for 15–20 minutes until the liquid has reduced slightly or crinkles up when put on an iced saucer. Or better still, use a sugar thermometer and when it reaches 108°C, 220°F, it is ready. Leave for 15 minutes to cool to ensure even distribution of fruit and bottle in warm, sterilized jars, and cover.

Undergraduate's room in Christchurch College, Oxford, 1867. (Photographer R. C. Gregg.)

BOOKMAKERS' SANDWICH

Epsom was first renowned for the mineral spring found there which made it a spa town in the 18th century. Epsom salts are named after the same spring. In 1780, the twelfth Earl of Derby founded the first Epsom Derby for three-year-old horses.

'When on public race days they (the downs) are covered with coaches and ladies, and an innumerable number of horsemen, as well gentlemen as citizens attending the sport. Then you drink the waters, or walk about as if you did; dance with the ladies . . , have music and company of what kind you like . . .'

Daniel Defoe, A Tour Through the Whole Island of Great Britain.

BOOKMAKERS' SANDWICH

This gargantuan sandwich is perfect for race-meetings, either for race-goers or bookmakers! The recipe was invented by Alfred Suzanne, chef to the Duke of Bedford in the 1890s.

700 g (1½ lb) sirloin or fillet of beef
a little salt
black freshly ground pepper
butter
made mustard and/or horseradish sauce
1 long, fresh, crusty loaf, such as a Vienna or thick French loaf

Serves about 4–6 depending on appetites

Season the steak with black pepper and grill it to your taste. When it is browned on both sides add a little salt.

Slice the loaf in half lengthways, butter it and reserve. Do not overcook the meat and, when ready, take it away from the grill and put on to a flat dish. Trim off any fat or gristle and put it, warm with the juices, on to one half of the buttered bread. Season and add the mustard and/or horseradish according to choice. Put the other half on and press down firmly.

Wrap in foil or waxed paper and put a light weight on top. When the loaf has cooled, unwrap and cut into thick slices, then wrap again in clean foil or paper.

Gammon steaks can also be used, or fried split kidneys and bacon, instead of the steak. With these latter a little home-made chutney can be added if liked.

Derby Day, Epsom, 1895.

TEA CAKE

Thomas Hardy was born at Higher Bockhampton, Dorset, and wrote many books set in Dorchester, such as The Mayor of Casterbridge *(1886) and other Wessex novels. In 1885 he settled at Max Gate, a house he designed himself, about a mile out of Dorchester. Puddletown, a few miles north-east of the town, was the setting for Weatherbury of* Far from the Madding Crowd *and Bathsheba Everdene's farmhouse is thought to be modelled on Waterston Manor, Lower Waterston, an Elizabethan house in the Piddle Valley.*

TEA CAKE

A recipe from Mrs Thomas Hardy, Max Gate, Dorchester.

450 g (1 lb) flour	2 teaspoons grated lemon rind
175 g (6 oz) dripping or butter, melted	1 egg, large
100 g (4 oz) sugar	a little milk

Pre-heat oven to 180°C, 350°F, Gas Mark 4. Lightly grease a baking sheet. Mix all dry ingredients together, then add the melted fat and mix well. Mix in the beaten egg and enough milk to make a firm but pliable dough. Put on to the sheet and bake for 45 minutes. Eat hot, with butter or jam.

MRS HARDY'S HOME-MADE SAUSAGE

450 g (1 lb) beef steak	$\frac{1}{2}$ teaspoon each of mace and nutmeg
450 g (1 lb) ham or lean bacon in the piece	salt and pepper
225 g (8 oz) breadcrumbs	2 eggs

Serves about 8

Mince the beef and ham very finely (about twice through a mincer or in a food processor) and mix together well. Then add the breadcrumbs, spices and seasonings. Bind with the eggs. Either roll or shape like a large sausage, tie up in a dampened cloth and boil in water for 3 hours, or bake it in a greased loaf tin for about 1½–2 hours. Leave to get cold before turning out. Then scatter with breadcrumbs, or pour over aspic to glaze it. Serve cold in slices. It is very good for a picnic or cold supper.

Thomas Hardy being honoured at Dorchester, Dorset, 1915.

TOAD-IN-THE-HOLE

Pangbourne is a boating village where the Thames is joined by the river Pang. The nautical training college was founded there in 1917 to train boys to become officers in the Merchant Navy and the Royal Navy. Pangbourne was the last home of Kenneth Grahame, the author of The Wind in the Willows.

TOAD-IN-THE-HOLE

This dish was often served at country hotels, or pubs, in the last century. Toad-in-the-Hole has deteriorated very much over the years. Up until the 1920s it was often made with good rump steak, chopped into pieces, sometimes with some kidneys added, but nowadays it is more often served made with sausages. It can be extremely good eaten piping hot from the oven.

675 g (1½ lb) pork sausages
225 g (8 oz) flour
pinch of salt

3 eggs
600 ml (1 pint) milk or milk & water

Serves 4

First grill the sausages under a hot grill, just until they are brown outside and half-cooked, they need not be cooked through. Set aside. Then mix the flour and salt, make a well in the middle and break the eggs into it with a little milk. Starting at the centre, work the flour into the eggs and milk until it is a smooth, thickish batter, then gradually add the milk or milk and water until it is creamy and of a pouring consistency, like a pancake batter.

Pre-heat the oven to 220°C, 425°F, Gas Mark 7. Well-grease a roasting pan and pour in a thin layer of batter, and put into the hot oven for about 5–7 minutes. Then take out, lay the sausages on top and pour the rest of the batter over them.

Bake in the oven about 35–40 minutes, towards the top of the oven, until the batter has puffed up and is crisp and brown around the edges. Serve at once.

Note: a few chopped, fresh herbs added to the batter gives a good flavour, also two or three grilled, chopped kidneys.

The Elephant Hotel, Pangbourne, Berkshire, c. 1892.

L OBSCOUSE

The steam ship Zealandic *had a gross tonnage of 10,898. She was 174 metres/477 feet long and was built at Harland and Wolff's yard at Belfast. The SS* Zealandic *was registered at Liverpool, owned by the Ocean Steam Navigation Company Ltd (Ismay, Imrie and Company).*

LOBSCOUSE

This is a very traditional Liverpool dish and the reason why 'scousers' or 'scouse' is a nickname for Liverpudlians. It is a beef stew usually served with pickled red cabbage, which cuts the richness. Salt beef was sometimes used at sea.

dripping or oil
1.1 kg (2½ lb) stewing beef, cubed, rolled in seasoned flour
450 g (1 lb) onions, coarsely sliced

225 g (8 oz) carrots, chopped
2 white turnips, chopped
700 g (1½ lb) potatoes, quartered
salt and pepper
stock to cover

Serves about 6

Put a little dripping or oil into a pan and quickly toss the beef cubes in it until brown all over. Transfer to a casserole or pan and add the vegetables with a little more oil or dripping, and just soften them. Season to taste. Add enough stock to cover the meat, bring to the boil, then simmer, and either cook on top of the stove for 2–3 hours, or bake in a slow oven (150°C, 300°F, Gas Mark 3). It is best left to cool, then any fat can be taken from the top when cold. It is almost better for re-heating.

PICKLED RED CABBAGE

1 medium head red cabbage
salt
white vinegar, about 600 ml (1 pint)

1 tablespoon sugar
1 tablespoon mixed pickling spice

Shred the cabbage fairly finely and take out stump. Lay on a flat dish, cover with salt and leave overnight. The next day, rinse and pack into jars. Boil up the vinegar, sugar and spices for 5 minutes, cool and pour over the cabbage to cover. Tie down and leave for at least one month before using.

Tenders leaving the quayside for the emigrant ship Zealandic *sailing on 4 October 1913 to Australia from Liverpool.*

ROAST VENISON

The name Sherwood comes from shire-wood, originally used for hunting by men of the shire. The Norman kings took it over as a royal forest and it was, of course, the home of the legendary Robin Hood and his Merry Men. At that time it covered over 10,000 acres of woodland and glades. The oaks were the predominant trees, most of them being taken for ship-building in later years, thus stripping the forest. However, several of the oaks achieved fame, especially the Major or Queen Oak, the meeting place of Robin Hood and his band, which still survives today at Bilhagh. It measures 30 feet around the trunk and has a circumference of almost 300 yards. The other famous oak is the Parliament Oak under which Richard II convened a parliament in the 14th century.

ROAST VENISON

Venison should always be marinated overnight, unless they are thin cutlets cut from a well-hung leg.

1 haunch venison or shoulder about 2.3 kg (5 lb)	1 rounded tablespoon flour squeeze of lemon
8 streaky bacon rashers	
½ teaspoon each of cinnamon & ginger	*Marinade*
	½ bottle red wine
1 teaspoon sugar	4 tablespoons olive oil
2 whole cloves & 4 whole allspice berries	1 sprig rosemary
	1 small sliced onion or shallot
¼ bottle claret or burgundy	1 bayleaf & 10 black
salt & pepper	peppercorns

The Parliament Oak, Sherwood Forest, Nottingham, 1880s.

Accompaniments
redcurrant or rowan jelly
chestnuts

Serves about 10

Marinate the joint in the above marinade overnight, turning over so that it is all covered. Lift out, pat dry a little and derind the rashers. Mix the ground spices together and rub them into the skin, sprinkle the sugar over and stick in the cloves and allspice. Then wrap the top over in the rashers and chop the rosemary over the top.

Put into the roasting tin with the claret or burgundy and strain about half the marinade over it. Cover with foil and roast at 200°C, 400°F, Gas Mark 6, for 30 minutes to the pound, turning down a little after the first hour. Put the cooked joint on a warmed dish and keep warm, reduce liquid to about half over a hot flame, then add the remaining strained marinade and the lemon juice. Boil this up, then cream the flour with a little water, add some of the hot gravy to this, then tip it in and stir until it is boiling and the sauce is slightly thickened. Serve separately in a sauce boat, also garnish with some fresh or canned, drained chestnuts which have been heated with a little butter and seasoned.

POTTED VENISON

This can be made from leftovers, by mincing it finely, mixing it with butter, seasonings and enough port or red wine to make a spreading paste. Seal with a layer of melted butter.

APPLE SHORTCAKE

Mr George Owen was noted throughout the world for his original work. He was particularly famous for perforated Ivory Porcelain.

Worcestershire is well known for hops, fruit and vegetables as well as its fine porcelain. The Vale of Evesham is famous for its Pershore plums and asparagus. It is also a cathedral city where, on St Catherine's Day, November 25th, the Dean and Chapter distributed the 'Cattern Bowl' of spiced wine. On November 23rd, St Clement's Day, young boys would go round singing:

Cattern and Clement comes year by year
Some of your apples and some of your beer,
Some for Peter and some for Paul,
Some for Him who made us all.
Peter was a good old man, for his sake give us some
Red apples and I'll be gone!

APPLE SHORTCAKE

100 g (4 oz) butter
75 g (3 oz) castor sugar
1 egg, beaten
175 g (6 oz) self-raising flour, sifted

225 g (8 oz) apple purée
castor sugar for sprinkling

Serves about 4

Cream the butter and sugar until light, then add the beaten egg and beat well together. Gradually add the sifted flour and mix in until it is a stiff dough. Do not add any liquid.

Light oven to 180°C, 350°F, Gas Mark 4. Grease a sandwich tin lightly. Roll the shortcake into 2 halves to fit tin and put one on the bottom. Spread the apple over, then put the other layer of short-bread on top. Bake in pre-heated oven for about 1 hour. When ready, take out and leave in tin to get cold, then cut into squares and sprinkle with sugar. Or serve it warm with cream.

SPICED WINE

12 whole cloves
pinch of grated nutmeg or small piece of mace
rind of ½ lemon, kept whole

2 bottles of claret or burgundy
2 wineglasses of port wine
sugar to taste
1 lemon, finely sliced

Serves about 15–20

Simmer the spices and lemon rind in 150 ml (¼ pint) water for 30 minutes, then strain into a bowl. Add the other ingredients, stirring well to dissolve sugar. Float lemon slices on top. Serve at room temperature. If wanted hot, heat up, but on no account let it boil or the alcohol content will evaporate.

Mr George Owen, artist potter at his workshop in the Royal Porcelain Works, Worcester, c. 1910.

LIGHT WIGGS

Newstead Abbey was formerly an Augustinian priory which became the Byron family home, inherited by him in 1798. Lord Byron lived there from time to time, but was forced to sell it on account of his debts, in 1816. There is a tomb to his favourite dog, Boatswain, in the grounds, to whom Byron wrote two poems.

Shade of heroes, farewell! your descendant departing
From the seat of his ancestors, bids you adieu!
Abroad or at home, your remembrance imparting
New courage, he'll think upon glory and you.
('On Leaving Newstead Abbey,' Lord Byron.)

Breakfast as a meal had quite changed in character from earlier centuries. In the country house it took place between nine and ten a.m. and usually consisted of tea, coffee, or chocolate with toast, rusks or little cakes.

LIGHT WIGGS

A very popular little yeasted cake, eaten for breakfast in the 18th century, which was quite rich as well as light. Recipe kindly given by Maggie Black, who adapted it from an 18th-century one.

225 g (8 oz) plain flour
1 teaspoon salt
pinch of mixed spice, optional
25 g (1 oz) fresh yeast, or 12 g (½ oz) dried yeast

50–75 g (2–3 oz) castor sugar
150 ml (¼ pint) tepid milk
75 g (3 oz) softened butter

Makes 8 Wiggs

Sift the flour with salt, and spices if using them, into a warmed bowl. Cream the yeast with 15 ml warm water and 1¼ teaspoons sugar, and when frothing, add the milk. Make a well in the flour, pour in the liquid and mix to a soft dough. Cover with buttered paper and leave in a warm place until doubled in bulk. Cream the remaining sugar and most of the butter and chill the mixture to firm it.

When the dough has risen, turn out on to a well-floured surface and roll or pat it into a rectangle about ½ cm (¼ in) thick. Dot it with one third of the butter/sugar mixture and fold into three as for flaky pastry. Repeat this twice more. Cut the final rectangle into 8 triangular wedges and put on a lightly buttered baking sheet, then leave to prove for 20 minutes. Pre-heat oven to 220°C, 425°F, Gas Mark 7. Brush tops with remaining butter and bake for 10–15 minutes. Cool on a rack.

HOT CHOCOLATE

Heat 600 ml (1 pint) milk, add 100 g (4 oz) chopped plain or bitter chocolate and stir. When melted, bring to simmering point and whisk for 3 minutes. Sweeten if liked. Pour hot and frothing into cups and top with whipped cream.

Lord Byron's bedroom, Newstead Abbey, Nottinghamshire, late 1880s. (Photographer, George Washington Wilson.)

FENLAND APPLE PIE

Ely was the great centre for basket-making right up until the 1950s. The great fen of Cambridgeshire was once a savage and trackless land of meres covering 680,000 acres. Ely, with its magnificent Norman cathedral, is still the dominating centre, although no longer an island. Hereward the Wake held out in the Isle of Ely against William the Conqueror long after the rest of England had surrendered. Until the 17th century, Fenland was sparsely inhabited by an independent race of people living in very primitive conditions, eating fish and fowl from the rivers and meres. In the 19th century, corn was reaped from platforms, the orchards picked from boats, boards were nailed to horse's hooves to prevent them sinking into the marshy land and the people walked on stilts. During hard winters the land was frozen over and the Fen people became excellent skaters, for it was a way of travelling over the long drains and rivers. It is said it was the only time the Fenmen did any visiting! They made their own skates from the leg bones of sheep to begin with. In 1870 a match was arranged between a skater and a train travelling from Littleport to Ely parallel to the river for 4 miles. The skater beat the train with time to spare! The Fenmen stayed as English champions until the 1930s.

After the snows came the floods, the last great one being in 1947. However, extensive drainage channels have been made to channel off the excess waters to reservoirs, an idea first suggested 300 years ago by a Dutch engineer called Vermuyden. So, at last, this great swamp is now the market garden of the south of England and is no longer famed as the area where the wildfowl fed on fish, nor, as Defoe writes in 1724:

'For carrying fish alive (to London) by land carriage; this they do by carrying great buts fill'd with water in waggons as the carriages draw other goods ... In these carriages they chiefly carry Tench and Pike, Perch and Eels, but especially Tench and Pike, of which here are some of the largest in England.'

FENLAND APPLE PIE

225 g (8 oz) shortcrust pastry (page 95)
450 g (1 lb) cooking apples, prepared
pinch of cinnamon & 2 cloves
25 g (1 oz) butter

50 g (2 oz) brown sugar
2 rounded tablespoons semolina
25 g (1 oz) currants
2–3 tablespoons black treacle or golden syrup

Serves 4–6

Roll out the pastry into 2 rounds of 20 cm (8 in) and line a pie plate with one. Cook apples with spices and butter until a pulp, then add sugar and semolina and cook for 5 minutes. Spread half, when cold, onto the pastry, add currants and treacle and the remaining apple pulp. Cover with pastry, press down and glaze with milk, then cook at 200°C, 400°F, Gas Mark 6 for 30 minutes.

Cutting and transporting the osiers in the fens for making into eel grigs, baskets, etc. On River Ouse, Ely, Cambridgeshire, 1895.

ECCLES CAKES

Blackpool has for many years been the resort chosen by most Lancashire people during Wakes week, when mills and factories close. Since the building of the famous tower it has produced every form of entertainment, but in this photograph it appears just a small seaside place.

It is well known for its Blackpool rock, a confection first made in the 19th century. It is made by boiling sugar and glucose, with two parts sugar to one part glucose and then it is poured on to a hot metal plate. It has a crunchy, crispy interior which is much enjoyed.

Eccles cakes are also a part of Wakes week.

With music and cakes
For to keep up the Wakes
Among wenches and fine country beaux

ECCLES CAKES

Eccles cakes are thought to have become known when the Puritans forbade the eating of rich cakes at religious festivals. The crisp pastry, filled with dried fruit and candied peel and spice, had some semblance of Christmas puddings or mincepies which somehow escaped notice and were allowed to be made.

450 g (1 lb) prepared puff pastry
175 g (6 oz) currants
50 g (2 oz) soft brown sugar
50 g (2 oz) mixed candied peel, chopped
25 g (1 oz) softened butter
pinch of nutmeg
1 egg white, lightly beaten
castor sugar to sprinkle

Makes about 14

Roll out the pastry to a thickness of 5 mm ($\frac{1}{4}$ in) and cut into 10 cm 4 in) rounds. Mix all the other ingredients together except the egg-white and sugar to sprinkle. Put a heaped teaspoon in the centre of each until all is used up. Dampen the edges with water and gather the edges together, pinching firmly to seal.

Light oven to 220°C, 425°F, Gas Mark 7. Turn the Eccles cakes over, so the fold is at the bottom, then roll lightly until the fruit is just showing through the pastry. Dampen the baking tray, score each cake across the surface twice and lay on the tray, not too close together. Paint over with the egg-white and sprinkle with sugar, then bake for about 20 minutes until the cakes are puffed and golden.

Blackpool beach, Lancashire, 1900.

DEVON JUNKET

Ilfracombe is the oldest of the north Devon resorts which is built in and among small hills, some of the beaches being reached by tunnels in the rocks. Devonshire junket was once popular at the seaside towns, and at the weekend it was a special family treat to go 'a-junketing'. It is usually made in a large china bowl, spread with clotted cream and sprinkled with spices.

DEVON JUNKET

600 ml (1 pint) creamy milk
1–2 tablespoons sugar, to taste
1 tablespoon brandy
1 teaspoon rennet essence or a
   junket tablet

225 g (½ lb) clotted cream
sprinkling of grated cinnamon
  or nutmeg

Serves 4

Heat the milk in a saucepan to blood heat, that is 36.90°C, 98.40°F. It must not be any hotter, or boiled and cooled, or it will not make. Pour the milk into a serving bowl, add the sugar and stir to dissolve. Add the brandy, and finally the rennet or junket tablet. This must be added last.

Leave the bowl undisturbed until it has set. Before serving, spread over carefully with the clotted cream and sprinkle with the cinnamon or nutmeg.

If clotted cream is not available, whipped cream can be substituted.

DEVON POT CAKE

This easily made cake is cooked in a frying pan and was often made for tea.

350 g (12 oz) flour
100 g (4 oz) butter or margarine
50 g (2 oz) lard
pinch of salt

100 g (4 oz) sultanas and
  currants, mixed
1 large egg, beaten
150 ml (¼ pint) milk, approx.

Fresh fruit, such as apples or blackberries, can be used in place of dried fruit. Mix together the egg and milk, beating well. Then mix the flour, butter, lard and salt together until quite amalgamated and like pastry. Then add the eggs and milk, mixing very thoroughly and finally add the fruit. Roll out to the size of the frying pan, about 20–23 cm (8–9 in), grease it well and put in the mixture. Cook slowly, browning well on both sides, or cook at 180°C, 350°F, Gas Mark 4 for 1 hour in the oven. When ready, take out, split open and spread with butter and brown sugar.

Stage-coach, Ilfracombe, Devon, c. 1900.

INDEX